Con[ ] Dyslexia

without losing the gift

Felicity Craig

Illustrated by Debbie Smith

ONE-TO-ONE Publications, Dartmouth

Published in 2004 by
ONE-TO-ONE Publications
33 Newcomen Road
Dartmouth, S. Devon
TQ6 9BN

British Library Cataloguing in Publication Data

A catalogue record for this book is available from the British Library.

ISBN 0 9520937 1 5 Paperback

Designed and produced by One-to-One Publications

Printed and bound in Great Britain by In-Focus Colour Printers
Totnes, Devon
Tel: 01803 867494

To the memory of Shona Larnie
1960 – 2004
Deputy Head of Longniddry Primary School
2000 – 2004
You passed on the magic of written language to
countless children,
and you will always live in their hearts.

ACKNOWLEDGEMENTS

To Nelson Thornes Ltd for permission to reproduce two passages from *Diagnostic and Remedial Spelling Manual* by Margaret Peters, ISBN 0 333 1555 48 (pp. 82 and 87).

Foreword

The teaching of literacy has been bedevilled for much too long by a bitter dispute between two opposing factions – those who advocate 'phonics first and fast', and those who insist rather on a 'whole language' approach ('real books', and reading for meaning and pleasure).

In *Conquer Dyslexia – without losing the gift,* I have been able to show that both sides are right in many important respects, for the simple reason that they are talking about different things. It is possible to see meanings in written words (without any necessary reference to spoken words). It is also possible to say written words aloud accurately (without necessarily having any idea what they mean). Both processes are vital; and both need to be developed, in all children, from the very beginning.

When we recognize this, we can direct a powerful searchlight into every previously murky corner in the literacy debate. We can explain word recognition and the true purpose of phonics. We can discover the best methods of teaching literacy (because they are the ways we have used from time immemorial to pass on the gift of spoken language).

And, by no means least, we can account for dyslexia. This is a condition which affects about ten to fifteen percent of the population (more males than females). It causes untold anguish for pupils and frustration for teachers. It blights lives and drains resources. It boosts our crime statistics and supplies our prisons. As a result, society is often denied the unusual talents, creativity and flair possessed by nearly all dyslexics.

But such waste can so easily be prevented. It has been my privilege, in writing the present book, to describe how this can be achieved. In the process, I hope that I have also been able to resolve the literacy battle, and show how both sides can work together for the good of all children.

So many people have cheered me along the way. I would like to pay particular tribute to Professor Robert Burden, who invited me to lecture at Exeter University on 'Understanding and Dealing with Dyslexia', and offer a 'Literacy Across the Curriculum' module to his post-graduate students. Longniddry Primary School made my phonics programme its own, and East Lothian Council went the second mile and published the whole thing in colour. Most of all the children themselves went on patiently showing me how their minds worked. That, and the unfailing support and encouragement of their parents, kept me going.

Contents

What is dyslexia?

Some children start sinking when they get to school.

Before school they have often been bright and breezy, fascinated by the way things work, doing wild and wonderful drawings, making great dinosaurs with their construction toys, or with plasticine, or with bits of card stuck together – anything they can get their hands on, really. Some of them do jigsaw puzzles wrong side up!

They can be wise beyond their years, taking in the grownups' conversation when you weren't aware they were listening, and interposing a comment or question at the end which shows they have understood absolutely *everything*. ('Mustn't discuss that again in front of Martin,' you say to yourself, as a result.)

They begin school full of hope and optimism. They are delighted with their new clothes and equipment. They like having a lunch box with delicious things to eat, and even more children to play with than there were at nursery.

And then – when is it that things start to go wrong? Looking back, it can be difficult to put your finger on the precise moment, because it happens only gradually.

It could be when the teacher shows them a word from a reading book they have never seen before. "What is it?" asks the teacher, "What does it say?" Martin stares at it in puzzlement, how can he possibly know? "But you knew it yesterday," declares the teacher, which is news to Martin. He stares desperately at the black pattern of squiggles in front of him, but it makes no sense. Helicopter? Rhinoceros? The air he breathes is suddenly thick with his worry, and his awareness of the teacher's disappointment.

It is a feeling which recurs as the other children look at the words in the book and identify them accurately, as if by magic. They press ahead, leaping from book to book, while Martin is stuck with the same one, which makes no more sense to him than it ever did.

It could be when the teacher berates him for forgetting his PE kit. "But it's Tuesday today," says the teacher crossly. "We always have PE on a Tuesday!" Tuesday? Today? Martin knows that Tuesday is one of the days of the week, but is very foggy about just when it occurs, or even that the days of the week *always happen in the same order.*

The other children can recite the days of the week – and the months of the year – and peculiar entities called multiplication tables, which never behave themselves for Martin. Why do his classmates know what to say, and the teacher smiles happily at them? They must be privy to some strange magic denied to Martin - because when he tries to do what they do, saying words or numbers that he thinks might fit, the teacher sighs, shaking her head. The air is thick for more and more of the time, and now the thickness rolls itself under a label, no one says it but Martin can feel it, it is 'Stupid'.

He must be stupid, if he cannot do what seems so frighteningly easy for everybody else.

Writing is a struggle, and Martin finds it difficult to distinguish between ordinary letters and capitals. His words are often spelled with capital letters in the middle, and instead of being pleased with him for getting the right letters, the teacher frowns (again) because *they are not written in the right way.* The right way? What is the right way? How is he even supposed to know that there *is* a right way and a wrong way?

But it gets worse. Letters not only transform themselves from capitals to ordinary ones and back again. They flip themselves over from left to right or from top to bottom, they play musical chairs with each other and turn up in words in entirely the wrong places, or even go missing altogether. The biggest bugbear of Martin's life turns out to be a procedure that once again the other children seem to master with the greatest of ease, but which may well blight Martin's existence well into adulthood and beyond. Very few dyslexics are free from its slimy coils, and many abandon the struggle to do it properly.

It is, of course, the procedure of *spelling*.

There is a way you are supposed to be able to learn to spell, called (Martin thinks) lookcoverwritecheck. You look at a word, cover it up, write it, and then check to see if you got it right. Martin tries very hard to do this, but it doesn't seem to work for him. His own spelling never matches the original; or, if it does, the word doesn't stick in his head, a week later it has jumbled itself up again into something completely different.

Copying from the blackboard is a nightmare for the same reason. You look at the words on the blackboard, then write them in your exercise book, then look back at the board for the next bit to write. But once again Martin's words never seem to match the ones he has just copied, and anyway how do you find your place on the blackboard when you don't recognize the words, and you have to keep looking up and down all the time?

Martin begins to dread going to school, because he feels so awful about himself when he is there. He may be very good at modelling and drawing, or making scenery and acting in plays. He may shine at sport or display a real talent for chess. But none of this seems to count or even to be noticed, it is just swamped by his inability to make any progress at all in the Academic Subjects.

Academic Subjects are based on reading, writing (both letters and numbers) and spelling. These procedures are only a way in to the content of the subjects, but because Martin has fallen at this very first procedural hurdle, the content – the real fun and excitement of academic subjects – is often beyond him: quite literally a 'closed book'.

Martin's difficulties form a pattern, and they have a name. There may be other features to the pattern (for example he might have trouble tying his shoelaces or catching a ball); but the main aspects cluster around his struggles with reading and writing. The 'lexicon', or collection of written symbols, is malfunctioning for Martin. It is going 'dys' – so his difficulties, and those of many many other children like him, are called 'dys-lexia'.

Secondary education

What is the prognosis as our young dyslexic labours through primary school and moves up to secondary education? Sadly, not very good. His problems might have been noticed at primary level, so he could be identified as having special educational needs – which in practice are met with some extra help from a classroom assistant. The teachers and support staff may or may not know that he is dyslexic and how this condition affects his ability to learn. Suddenly there is even more reading to do, even more writing, even more copying from the blackboard – and much more homework, which he often doesn't understand. He could spend hours producing a couple of paragraphs when the teacher wanted a couple of pages. Most of his work seems to come back with the same sort of comments written at the bottom: 'You need to work on your spelling and punctuation.' How is he supposed to do that? It is like asking him to climb Mount Everest without oxygen, he is just as well equipped.

Some teachers expect him to share the reading aloud in class, and the silence is dreadful while he stumbles over the simplest words. He can only guess what the silence means – irritation? pity? – embarrassment? He wishes he were anywhere else rather than in this place, surrounded by these people, faced with this never-ending succession of tasks he cannot do.

So, increasingly, he takes himself somewhere else. School holds nothing positive for him, only humiliation. He sets off in the morning, but does an about-turn before he reaches the school gates, and spends his day on the streets instead. Doing – what? Does he feel a debt to society, that has given him so little? Some mindless graffiti may help him to feel a shade better about himself, followed by a bit of shoplifting. But the streets are beset with dangers in their turn, he is an easy prey for the drug pedlars, and it is only a short step from sampling drugs to becoming hooked. Then he has to embark on more serious crime to feed his habit, and almost inevitably ends up doing his first stretch in custody.

Some years ago, Channel 4 examined the incidence of dyslexia among inmates in a Young Offenders Institution in Scotland. Normally dyslexia affects only 10 to 15 percent of the population as a whole – and that was what the researchers expected to find. To their surprise nearly *half* the inmates turned out to be dyslexic!

But given the scenario described in the preceding pages, it is their surprise that is surprising. The only puzzle is that any dyslexics survive school and go on to lead creative, fulfilling lives – but many do. Our job, surely, is to help bring that about for all dyslexics, not just some of them.

Another noteworthy feature is the gender of the dyslexic population. Girls can suffer severely from the condition; but they seem to be in a minority. Over the years, I would say that for every two girls coming to me for help, I have worked with at least eight males.

So as we survey each September's new entrants to Reception classes up and down the country, knowing that some of them are likely to struggle in the same way as Martin, we need to keep another fact in mind.

Very often, these children are boys.

6   What is dyslexia?

II

The roots of language

tallying   ratio

adding and subtracting

operating on sets

HCF & LCM

X+Y=Z

learning and remembering

A personal history

I didn't start out with an interest in dyslexia as such. I have always been passionate about reading and writing, mainly because these two activities transformed my own childhood.

Naturally I don't remember learning to understand spoken language, and to talk, or even learning to read (in any great detail); but I remember the books I read. They were all magic. I was a sickly child and had frequent bouts of bronchitis, which meant spending weeks in bed, laboriously wheezing away until my chest had cleared, and the doctor pronounced me fit to get up again. This was long before the days of television or even radio: what we had when I was little was a wireless, and that was a big cumbersome object which lived downstairs. No one would have dreamed of transporting it up to my bedroom. But we had books in abundance. Every room, including mine, had a bookcase, crammed with all manner of treasures about any imaginable subject. So although physically I was confined to a narrow bed, in a narrow room, with only the firelight dancing on the ceiling for company, in every other sense I was as free as a bird: exploring the lands at the top of the Faraway Tree, wandering through Sherwood Forest with Robin Hood and Maid Marian, or roaming around in Camelot and sharing their quests with Arthur's Knights of the Round Table.

These worlds were as real to me as my mattress and pillows, mustard poultices and regular spoonfuls of medicine – perhaps even more real, I certainly spent most of my time there, and left them reluctantly when I had to eat my dinner, or expose my back and chest to the doctor's cold, unfriendly stethoscope.

Little black squiggles, arranged in serried rows on white or creamy paper, were my passport to these enchanted worlds. I never questioned how such trifling things could work such marvels, how it was that they seemed to become transparent while I looked at them, so that I was hardly aware of the squiggles themselves, only the places I stepped into through the words. In some strange way the words created the worlds I travelled to – or rather helped me to create them – or rather helped me to share in a process of creation with whoever it was who had put those squiggles on the page in the first place. I never had to learn that language was a creative medium, that was a fact of my experience which seemed as instinctive and natural as breathing. (Also, given my circumstances, a good deal easier and more comfortable.) Language – written words – were things that other people had used to weave rich and wonderful tapestries, and which spread these tapestries in front of me, so that I could share them too.

I remember bits of learning to read. I remember running to my mother with the very first book I ever read by myself, I don't know what it was called or what it was about, but it was all of six pages long, and had a cover of pink card. "Mummy, Mummy, Mummy – I'm on page four!" My mother celebrating with me my delight in my achievement. Another time when I was forced to miss school because of the familiar bronchitis, a close family friend who was herself a teacher came to visit. As usual I had my nose in a book. "What do you do, Flicky, when you come across a word you don't know?" she asked curiously. I tried to think. "I just skip over it and go on to the next one," I finally decided. But I remember learning phonics at school, during the interludes of health when I could be part of the clanging, bustling confusion along with all the other non-wheezing children. I don't remember learning the sounds of the alphabet, but I remember phonic reading books, satisfying lists of words that all had the same sound, and when I knew those, oh joy, I would be put on to the next book in the series. Real books, of course, were at home; and what I had told the family friend was true, but only part of the truth. Once I had come across a new word several times, then, eventually, I would stop and look at it, fit sounds to the letters, and work out how to say it.

It seemed that I had become a fluent reader in spite of my long absences from school – or even, perhaps, because of them. Certainly I had no difficulty 'catching up' when I did put in an appearance at school. Any subject that was wheeled out dressed in written language fell into my hands, so that far from being behind in such subjects, I was in fact ahead.

I was aware that reading did not come nearly so easily to some of my classmates, and I remember being perplexed when they stumbled and lurched their way through a page of print that was wholly transparent to me. How could it be so difficult? How could they not see what the words meant and said, as soon as look at them? What was getting in their way, and why did they continually fall foul of such invisible barriers? It made little sense to the child I was then, I had no idea that one day I would be able to look inside those children's heads and describe those barriers, so as to make them real and comprehensible to everyone else who, like me, can take reading for granted.

Just as I do not remember much about learning to read, I have only vague memories of learning to write, but I remember vividly the day I became a writer. My father had been listening to me wittering on, and decided, as only a fond parent could, that what I had been saying was not childish prattle at all, but immortal verse. So he sat down at his typewriter, and lo and behold, the words that had come out of my head appeared on the flimsy sheet of typing paper before him, in deep blue print. I can remember the look of the typed words, and the feel of the paper: I can almost remember its smell. The last line in each verse was about twice as long as the others, stretching near to infinity across the page, and declared:

'But best of all I like to see all the birds singing in a tree.'

I hope that I have written a small amount of real poetry since then. But no writing I have formed myself has ever filled me with such an electric sense of wonder and exaltation as that very first sight and feel of my own words in print. They were out there and visible, just like real book words, they were mine, and they would last forever. Written words were not just things that other people could inscribe on paper. I could become one of those people; I could generate these powerful entities myself, and so, in my turn, share with others the creation of new worlds that we could all explore together.

My horizon exploded in that instant. Nothing would ever be the same again, not now I had learned that I too could one day put pen to paper, I too could make things with written words, I too could be an author.

So, since growing up, my purpose as a teacher has been very clear. Because reading and writing have always been such magical experiences for me, I have wanted to secure a passport to that magic world for all children, without exception, no matter what the barriers in their way might be.

Engaging with language

Long before written language, there was spoken language. We tend to think that it was invented for purely utilitarian reasons – so that we could communicate with each other, explain how to use tools, how to hunt the animals we needed for food, clothing and shelter, and therefore have a better chance of surviving in the great struggle for existence.

But it is likely we had a far profounder purpose than that. If you observe a baby's early engagement with language, her initial interest is almost always awakened by the *names* of things she encounters. For instance, before my elder daughter began to speak, I remember disputing with her Dad about whether her first word would be 'Ma-ma' or 'Da-da'. In the event, it was 'Doey', the name of the dog, which put both of us in our place! Helen obviously knew what she meant by the word. She said it when the dog came into the room, and she leaned towards him, waving her arms about, and chuckling with satisfaction. The dog's name was 'Joey', and 'Doey' was the closest she could get at her first attempt. She must have heard the word 'Joey' many times, though, and learned that it referred to the dog, before she could use 'Doey', as the dog's name, herself.

Then when my daughter Gwynneth was fifteen months old, we came home to England for the first time since her birth, and stayed for some weeks with my husband's parents. English houses were a totally new experience for Gwynneth, and the kitchen especially intrigued her. One evening she demanded my attention after her tea, while she lurched uncertainly from item to item, smacking it with her hand, and saying enquiringly, "Dis?" "Sink." "Dis?" "Bowl." "Dis?" "Stove." "Dis?" "Cupboard." "Dis?" "Table." "Dis?" "Chair." "Dis?" "Sink." "Dis?" "Bowl." "Dis?" "Stove." "Dis?" "Cupboard." And so on, with great glee, round and round, soaking it all in, quivering in her determination to organize her small world, not stopping to say the words herself, but grabbing all the names she could for all the objects within sight and reach. After about fifteen minutes I had to go and do something else: Gwynneth could have gone on indefinitely.

My daughters are typical rather than unusual. Most babies have a comparable passion for names, and there is a very good reason for this. What impels them at first is not the desire to communicate (that will come later). No, they are determined to make *sense* of their experience, to notice the similarities and differences between objects, so as to learn which ones can be grouped together under the same 'heading' (chair, table, window, door, plate, bowl, knife, spoon, wall, ceiling, shoes, trousers, shirt, dress, carpet, fire, stove, cushion, curtain, tree, bush, grass, flower...). They need to make increasingly fine distinctions in order to learn these names – to register the difference between chairs and tables, knives and spoons, plates and bowls, trees and bushes: then they can label the objects accurately.

Similarly, when as adults we embark on a new field of study – identifying birds for example – we find it intensely satisfying to be able to distinguish between various birds of prey, or different kinds of sparrows, or finches. To begin with they are all 'birds' – feathered creatures with beaks, two legs and wings. Those features are constant and must always be present if the creature is to be called a 'bird'. Soon we learn to group 'birds' under fairly broad headings: waterfowl, birds of prey, owls, small songbirds. But before long, we can name buzzards and eagles, tree sparrows and house sparrows, or distinguish a goldfinch from a chaffinch. The more skilled we become at this process, the more we feel we are on the road to mastery of the subject. This feeling is well justified, because in order to identify birds accurately, we have to observe them in ever greater detail, always noticing what makes individuals like other birds, and what makes them different.

Babies are learning in the very same way, with insatiable hunger for the detail which will enable them to do so. They are continually filing objects under any number of headings in their minds, quite effortlessly, so long as we provide the names, in conjunction with their experience, whenever those names are needed.

Language and mathematics
The process of assigning names to objects represents a deeply mathematical way of thinking!

In order to appreciate this, let's imagine a child who has learned to understand the word 'chair', so clearly that if you show her a small doll's chair, with a rounded back and blue legs, and say to her "What is it?" she will immediately reply, "It's a chair."

How does she know? Perhaps she has never seen such a small chair before, or one with that sort of back and legs of that particular colour. But she identifies it without hesitation. So what mental procedures underlie her confident assertion?

To begin with, she has to take note of the word 'chair', it has to register. Her mum comes home, and with a sigh and a cup of tea sinks into an arm chair. Her dad leaves his glasses on the rocking chair and the dog sits on them. When it is time for her to have her meals with everybody else, she graduates from her high chair to a proper dining chair.

The interesting thing about all these chairs is that they are really quite different from each other. A plump and squashy arm chair bears little resemblance to a lean and portable dining chair. And yet each of the objects is labelled with a pattern of sounds that is in every case the same.

The child finds this intriguing. Why is the pattern of sounds always the same? And she starts to notice the similar features of these different objects, so as to identify the common 'factors' of 'chairness'. All 'chairs', she observes, have a seat designed for only one sitter, they have some sort of a base which rests on the floor, and they have a back for leaning against. If one of these factors is missing, a back for instance, then whatever-it-is might still be sat upon, but is not a 'chair' and has to be given another name instead.

How old is this child? She may be less than one – she is almost certainly less than two.

Yet without instruction of any kind, she has just engaged in a process which is at once highly abstract and passionately creative. Never mind that each separate chair is particular and tangible. The child's concept of 'chairness' is abstracted from her awareness of all the different chairs in her experience. It is not a thing at all. It is an idea in her head, and she has created it herself.

This has happened in strict accordance with the laws of logic and mathematics. An object cannot be a 'chair' unless it has all the essential features; so these essential features, taken together, constitute the 'highest common factor' of chairness. The idea takes shape as a child hears the word alongside all the different objects which can bear that word as a name. And she is not performing this feat for just one set of objects. The highest common factors for every group of items in her experience continually crystallize out; and as she forms the concepts, she labels them, she flings a border around each one so as to keep it whole, a border which is one of the most powerful intellectual tools imaginable, a simple pattern of sounds which she uses as a name.

Babies are not merely identifying the highest common factors of sets of objects, however. While she has been abstracting the factors essential to chairness, our miniature Einstein has also been noticing the uncommon factors which are present in some chairs and not in others. Chairs can be different colours; some can have arms; some have four legs, others just one in the middle, and some have legs ending in rockers. They can be made of wood or plastic or metal and be covered with material; they can be soft and comfortable or hard and forbidding. All these factors, too, are combined with her recognition of the essential ones, and form her total conception of 'chairs-in-general'. So her use of the word 'chair' is not only an acknowledgement that the object named embodies the 'highest common factors' of chairness. The word also summons up for her all the characteristics of all the chairs she has come across, and is therefore the 'lowest common multiple' of these characteristics.

We could express this in terms of a classic Venn diagram. Let's suppose that a baby has encountered three different chairs in her life so far: A) a wooden high chair, painted blue; B) a stained wooden dining chair with a cushion on it, and C) a blue upholstered arm chair. Each chair can be regarded as a 'set' containing all the characteristics of that particular chair, and this may be represented diagrammatically as follows:

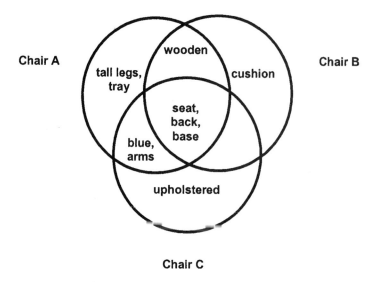

Chair C

The factors which are common to all three chairs are the seat, the back and the base, so these factors form the intersection of the three sets, and help the baby to construct her central concept of chairness. In addition, she has learned that some chairs are blue, can be made of wood, have tall legs, trays or cushions, and be upholstered, with arms in one or two cases. These factors, taken together with the intersection of the sets, form the union of the sets, and constitute the 'lowest common multiple' of chairs in general, as she has experienced them so far. When she encounters further chairs, for example a metal chair on a swivel base, the intersection of the sets will stay the same, but the lowest common multiple will expand to take account of the new characteristics.

This is just what happens when we are dealing with the factor structure of numbers:

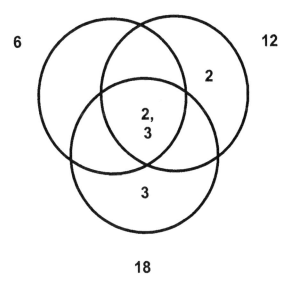

The prime factors which are common to all three numbers are 2 x 3 (= 6): the intersection of the sets. The non-common factors (another 2 and another 3), multiplied with 6, form the union of the sets, and generate the lowest common multiple of the three numbers (36). If another number with the same HCF (e.g. 24) is included in the picture, the lowest common multiple expands to include the non-common factor from 24 (another 2) and becomes 72.

Viewed in this way, it might even seem easier to perform the operations with numbers than with the characteristics of various objects! Not to worry – our baby certainly doesn't, and is soon a dab hand at noticing all the varied differences in detail which will allow her to classify everything she experiences into sets – and so impress her own personal order onto what seemed at first like chaos.

It looks as if the process underlying language is not so much the ability to manipulate sounds, but to form abstract concepts, and to move sets of ideas around inside your head. The pattern of sounds which is used as a name for a particular group of ideas (e.g. 'chair') is really no more than a convenience, a unifying focus enabling a baby to combine the elements in her concept and think of it as a unit. The word is a peg where the concept can be safely stored, and which allows for swift retrieval when that concept needs to be thought about.

More mathematical thinking

So, just in order to understand and use names, a small child is operating on sets, and appreciating the highest common factors and lowest common multiples of those sets.

But she is also employing many more mathematical processes as she takes possession of the world of language. Long before she has uttered a single word herself, she has been engaging in what is probably the most basic mathematical procedure of all – that of *tallying*.

We used tallying to help us count before numbers were invented. A shepherd boy could 'count' his sheep by matching each sheep with a notch carved on a stick. Any unmatched notches at the end of the day meant that number of missing sheep, and he had to find them before settling down for the night. Only when each notch was paired off with its missing sheep could he relax.

Counting is just one application of this incredibly useful procedure. In essence, tallying consists of associating two items as a pair, and we cannot even begin to think without forming such associations. A baby associates the smell of milk with the taste and feel of it in her mouth, and all these things with a nice full tummy. Soon the sight of her mother's face is linked with the same experiences. She associates the sound of water running out of a tap with the excitement of having a bath; wearing a jacket and hat with going outdoors; sitting in a high chair with eating; cups with drinking, and spoons with more solid food. The list is endless. Whenever a baby shows expectations of some kind, this has to mean that she has previously formed an association between whatever it is she is expecting, and the event which is prompting that anticipation. She has tallied the two things in her mind, so that now the occurrence of one of those two things automatically implies the other.

The association is always between just two items to begin with, but more associations can then be formed with either one of the initial pair, so the baby is soon building up clusters – or *sets* – of ideas which are all linked with each other.

Words may be thought of as sets of sounds which can be tallied with each other, and added to or subtracted from other sets of sounds so as to alter their meanings. For instance, a child differentiating between the two words 'pig' and 'pin' tallies the 'pŭ' and 'ĭ' sounds from each word with each other. These are 'common factors' and 'cancel out'. The *un*common factors are the 'gŭ' sound in 'pig' and the 'n' sound in 'pin' – so these are what distinguish the words from each other, and allow her to assign separate meanings to the two words.

Uncommon factors can be added or subtracted in other ways to indicate a change of meaning. Suppose that a child is learning to understand the word 'smile'. Her mother picks her up, with a broad smile on her own face, and says encouragingly, "Smile!" The youngster smiles back at Mum, and gradually learns that the set of sounds 'smile' not only refers to the happy sort of feeling which moves your lips upwards: it is also a request. When you say 'smile' to someone you want them to perform the action.

Mum reads her a bedtime story, and they come across a picture of a rag doll wearing a broad grin. "Look," says her mother, "dolly is smiling."

In order to identify the difference in meaning between the two words 'smile' and 'smiling', the child has to notice that the set of sounds 'smile' is common to both words, and carries the same root meaning of bending your mouth around in a happy sort of way. The difference between the two sets is the 'ing' ending. Attach that to the set of sounds 'smile' and you change the force of the word. From being a request it becomes a description. So 'smile' plus 'ing' equals a new word, 'smiling'. 'Smiling' minus 'ing' equals a different word, 'smile'.

She discovers that you can do this with any number of words: in no time she is adding and subtracting prefixes and suffixes all over the place, so as to modify the meanings of the words she is learning to understand and to say.

As the child moves on increasingly to talking herself, and stringing her own words together to generate spoken sentences, it becomes obvious that still more intelligent procedures are coming into operation. Have a look at some of the things older children are saying – four and five year olds: much more accomplished talkers now, but still barely school age.

For example, when Gwynneth was four, she declared thoughtfully one day that our breadcrumbs were great big loaves to dollies. My niece Susan, at five, made an equally exciting discovery. "Do you mean," she said to her mother, "that my Granny is your Mummy?"

What delights both Gwynneth and Susan is an appreciation of similarities – but it is not two objects they have identified as similar. What is the same in both cases is the relationship. Loaves are to people as breadcrumbs are to dolls. Grannies are to mothers as mothers are to children.

This is the mathematical concept of ratio. Again, it is a highly abstract concept, and again small children are forming it over and over without difficulty. Listen to any young child, and you will discover the idea of ratio is quite central to her thinking. It is, in fact, a very important means by which she orders her experience. She soon comes to realize that things have to be fitting. Her own clothes, shoes, gloves, wouldn't do for Mum. Miniature tea sets are satisfying because they go with the size of the dolls. A throne in a giant's castle is as much a chair as the smaller version in her own home: it is just scaled up in ratio to the size of its occupant. Some tools (e.g. knives and forks) are appropriate to some activities (eating); whereas buckets and spades are what you need for building sand castles. It is no semantic accident that we call ourselves *ratio*nal beings, for this appreciation of ratio – what is fitting, what is appropriate, what goes with what, and how – is fundamental to all our thought processes, and our acquisition of language. We would be unable to learn language at all without using this concept, because the relationship between any word and the idea it represents is the same as the relationship between all other words and their meanings. Unless we understand this, we cannot grasp the purpose of the myriads of sound patterns we are busily storing in our minds.

The more we examine these comparisons between language and mathematical thinking, the more apparent it becomes that the acquisition of language is an amazingly clever process. We haven't properly acknowledged this before because we tend to take learning language for granted, without examining the mental processes which must be fundamental to it.

It is fascinating to pursue this line of enquiry by noticing a child's *mistakes*. Mistakes are interesting because they are not copied from other people, they are the child's own invention – and therefore tell us a great deal about how the child's mind is working.

Gwynneth, again, at four, intrigued us all because she persisted in saying "I have tooken," rather than "I have taken." If you examine the logical patterns of thought which have culminated in this construction, they are quite staggering.

For a start, she already knew how to form the past tense of words like 'jump', 'skip', 'walk', etc. – just stick a sharp 'd' sound on the end. To form the perfect tense, you put a 'have' in front of the past tense, making forms like 'I have jumped', 'I have skipped'. (She didn't explain what she was doing to herself, she merely went ahead and did it.)

She was also aware that not all verbs make their past and perfect tenses in this way. Some change the vowel sound instead, so 'I get' changes to 'I got' and 'I have got'. 'I sit' changes to 'I sat' and 'I have sat'.

Some words, though, like 'wake' and 'break', change the vowel sound to make the past tense ('I woke', 'I broke') and then you have to tack on the suffix 'en' to get the perfect tense ('I have woken', 'I have broken').

She must have worked out that this is what has to be done, because she has constructed the form 'I have tooken' by analogy with forms like 'I have woken' and 'I have broken'. She hasn't come up with 'I have tōken' (which would be an analogy by rhyme). Instead, she has identified the past tense, 'took', and added the suffix 'en' to that past tense form, so as to construct what seems to her a completely logical perfect tense. She has abstracted the idea and force inherent in the vowel change and in the suffix 'en', and she has applied those ideas in a construction which is entirely of her own making.

In this instance, she is thinking algebraically. She may not have the words for 'verb', 'past tense', 'perfect tense' – but she does have the concepts. She has arranged these concepts in her mind in an algebraic formula. 'X' is the concept of the past tense. 'Y' is the pattern of the pre-word 'have' and the suffix 'en'. 'Z' is the concept of the perfect tense. The formula $X+Y=Z$ works when you substitute the past tense of verbs like 'break' and 'wake', so it's reasonable to suppose that it will also work if you substitute the comparable form of 'take'...

Now find any four-year-old, record her mistakes – and analyse the mental processes underlying those mistakes. I guarantee you will revise your assumptions about the level of intelligent thought taking place in that small head, quite matter of factly and unobtrusively.

As an integral part of their ability to use spoken language, children must also be handy at sequencing and organizing, and have excellent memories. Spoken English uses about forty-four different sounds all told, but those forty-four sounds can be arranged in such an infinity of different ways that we can generate hundreds and thousands of words, and still find new sound patterns when new concepts arise and need words to represent them. A spoken word is a particular arrangement of sounds. The only difference between many words is that their constituent sounds are differently arranged, and most children can appreciate this with no trouble. Words like 'spill' and 'lips', 'cat' and 'tack', 'carts' and 'stark', 'pain' and 'nape', use the same sounds, but are rarely confused because the sounds emerge in a different order. Some words may be muddled when a child is first learning them, but are soon sorted out: they have to be if the child is going to be understood by her family and peers. So the awareness and learning of different sound sequences is, once again, fundamental to our use of language; and we have to have first-rate memories if we are going to be able to store all these different sound patterns.

Similarly, spoken sentences are particular arrangements of words, and the order of those words is vital to the meaning of the sentence. 'Man bites dog' conveys a different meaning altogether from 'dog bites man'; saying 'my toy fire engine was under the chair' is not the same as saying 'the chair was under the toy fire engine'. Children soon become very good at organizing their words so as to convey the right meaning, which shows us that they are very good at organizing their thoughts in a logical way, and making sure that the order of their words reflects that logical organization.

What I have tried to show is that these sophisticated mental processes – tallying, adding and subtracting, operating on sets, identifying the highest common factors and lowest common multiples of groups of ideas, appreciating ratio, thinking algebraically, sequencing and organizing sounds and words, as well as the ability to learn and remember – are not 'optional extras': they are essential to language. We cannot use language, to any extent, without employing all these processes. Because we need them to acquire language in the first place, they cannot be taught (since language would be required to teach them), so they must be innate, already in place at birth, waiting only for the relevant experiences which will bring them into play.

Moreover, it is very important to recognize that just because a child is having difficulty with spoken language, this does not necessarily mean she is lacking in these fundamental abilities. She may be; but equally there could be many other reasons for her poor showing (e.g. physical or sensory impairments of some kind). We are never entitled to assume that the intelligence isn't there, because no 'test' ever devised can prove the absence of intelligence. We can legitimately expect such tests to demonstrate the *presence* of that valuable commodity, but not the reverse; you can never prove conclusively that something does not exist!

Anyway, it is much more positive and exciting to assume that the intelligence is there, in every single child, and to devise educational programmes which will allow that intelligence to flourish. Then no child will be limited by the poverty of our own expectations.

Learning to talk

Another reason that we have been inclined to overlook the advanced intellectual procedures basic to acquiring language is that most studies of children learning language have focused largely on when they begin to speak. It seems easier to measure and record their first utterances than it does to identify the moment when they understand their first word. How do we know whether they are understanding or not?

This isn't a real problem, however. We may not know just when comprehension first occurs, but we do know, without a shadow of a doubt, that it does occur – and that understanding a word must logically precede a child's ability to use that word meaningfully herself. It is perfectly legitimate, scientifically speaking, to record a child's observed behaviour, and to draw conclusions from that behaviour about the patterns of thinking which must have gone before.

So any study of language should properly begin, not with speaking, but with *hearing*. Children's ability to talk must emerge from an extensive understanding of the language they hear, developed in very much the sorts of ways I have just described. Learning to understand language is a creative process, because the child is constructing her own meanings for the words she hears; but her meanings are not arbitrary, they coincide with the meanings assigned to the same words by the people she hears talking. Learning language means entering into a consensus with other speakers of her native tongue that their words will share a common meaning: that their concepts of coatness, doorness, shoeness, underness, overness, will be pretty much the same. This is why children of English speaking parents grow up speaking English, French children speak French, German children speak German. Language is a common heritage which enables people to share their thoughts – you can use words in the confident expectation that the meanings they represent for you will be the same meanings they represent for other people. Words are physical constructs, faithfully reflecting the movements of our minds, and therefore laden with the meanings we have imparted to them. But because they are physical constructs, they can be perceptible to others, and so become a meeting place where thoughts can coincide, and be experienced in the same way by different thinkers. Little wonder that language is often regarded as the crowning achievement of the human race!

Children are not long content with the mere ability to understand what they hear. There comes a moment for nearly every youngster when she realizes she can produce words herself. The noises issuing from her mouth are just like the noises coming into her ears, and so can be charged with the same meanings.

This is almost certainly a chance realization at first. A baby starts babbling, at about five months, because vocalizing is fun, not because she is consciously embarking on the first stage in learning to talk.

There she is, stuck in her cot with nothing much to do. She has exhausted the possibilities of her rattle and her mobile, and she can't go exploring as she hasn't yet perfected the crawl. Life is looking distinctly boring, when it dawns on her that she has a custom made plaything literally under her nose. As she waggles her lips and tongue, these rather interesting noises come out.

To begin with, she probably doesn't recognize that she is producing the sounds herself. But quite soon she notices that the same sounds happen whenever she has the same feelings in her mouth and voice. This is a very exciting discovery. It means that she can produce sounds at will. When she pulls her lips apart, with a bit of voice behind them, a rather nifty 'bŭ' sound emerges. And if she does it again, the same thing happens! Very satisfying. Waggling things around at the back of her throat produces a nice gooey sound, and there seem to be all sorts of noises she can make with her tongue. Perhaps life has possibilities after all.

Once again, what the baby is doing is tallying. She is matching items of sense data in pairs – the sound of a 'b' with the feeling of producing it; a 'gŭ' sound with its matching vocal sensation, and so on. Only when these associations have been firmly made can she begin to imitate sounds. Her mother leans over her cot, going 'ba – ba – ba' in the inane way mothers have, and she finds this delightful because the sounds her mother is making are just like the sounds she has already learned to make herself. (Her mother, at first, is imitating her!) So she can go 'ba – ba – ba' in reply. The two of them can have a fine old time, going 'ba – ba – ba' and 'gu – gu – gu' at each other for minutes on end. Even better: her babbling game has now spread out to include someone else.

In the meantime, and as a separate process, the baby has been learning that noises can be words – they can convey meanings. And some of these words she has produced herself, quite by accident. One day it dawns that if a particular pattern of sounds, coming out of her own mouth, is very like a pattern of sounds bearing its cargo of meaning into her ears, she too can invest that pattern of sounds with the same meaning. She too can utter it as an undivided whole and think the meaning through it. It is no longer a random pattern of sounds; now, it has become a word. Now, she is not just babbling any longer: now, she can talk.

Her first words are only close approximations of the words she hears, as my daughter Helen's first word was 'Doey', not 'Joey'. This is because she is seizing on heard words which most closely resemble her own chance utterances. She is not yet concerned about reproducing words exactly. What fills her whole world is the realization that these constructs which she herself has produced can be charged with meanings. As a result, she can control the meanings she makes far more powerfully than when she was only listening. She can say words herself whenever she pleases, and therefore summon up their meanings at will. Language has become a possession, and she begins to perceive that she can use it as she wants and when she wants. Few discoveries she makes in later life will be more intoxicating than this one.

So, as long as her own words are fairly close to the ones used by other people, that is all that matters at first. 'Doey' sounds like

'Joey' and can name the same animal; 'da-da' sounds like 'daddy', 'lellow' like 'yellow', 'blana' like 'banana'.

This undertaking soon spreads out to the point where she can string words together, and produce quite reasonable sentences. Again, her early sentences are nothing like a meticulous copy of the 'grown-up' ones. She knows that words can be arranged in sequences to represent physical events, and fastens on just the salient features of those physical events, at first. 'See big plane' names all the important elements in a particular happening. In addition, the words follow the conventional English order, so can function as a perfectly acceptable sentence, quite sufficient for her present purposes. But if the adult she is talking to responds, "Yes, I can see the big plane," this helps her to register the intervening words which establish the meaning of the proposition even more precisely. Gradually, she learns to interpose such 'between' words herself, so as to make sure that her meaning cannot be misunderstood.

Her early approximate versions of individual words are discarded as well. 'Lellow' doesn't sound exactly like the word she hears and needs a bit of adjustment if it is going to be a faithful reproduction. In order to achieve this, she has to listen closely to the word, and isolate the first sound in her mind. A 'yu' sound matches with a different vocal sensation from 'lu', so if she substitutes the 'yu' feeling, she should produce the 'yu' sound. Got it! Now 'yellow' sounds right, just like the proper word.

As she determines to go on making her words 'sound right', she discovers that this same process can be used whenever she learns to say a new word. She can get it right at her first attempt if she listens closely to the word. She isolates the initial sound and matches it with the appropriate vocal sensation, then the next sound, then the next and the next, tallying heard sounds with vocal sensations all the way along the word. In this manner her language coincides ever more closely with the language she hears, until her pronunciations as well as her sentence structure are virtually indistinguishable from everybody else's.

She has indeed claimed her membership of the human race. She can understand the language she hears, so long as it is relevant to her own experience. She can talk herself, using words to represent the same meanings, and organizing her sentences in the same way, as those around her. But she can also arrange those words so as to express ideas which are original with her, new and fresh minted as a bright pound coin. Language is at once a common heritage and a unique possession, enabling us to share our world with each other, and to articulate that world in ways that have never been thought or said before.

III

Language through the looking glass

Beginning the journey

Three books have shaped my thinking about language. I read the first when I was studying for my BA degree at a liberal arts college in America (Salem College in Winston-Salem, North Carolina).

Courses in an American college are organized on the basis of three hour-long lectures each week. These lectures are informal, and the groups attending are fairly small – more like a British A level class. During these classes, we took notes and discussed, and in our own time read the assigned books. In addition, each of us was given some outside reading to do, and by the end of the semester we had to produce a term paper about what we had read.

For one of my philosophy courses, I was asked to read *Philosophy in a New Key: A Study in the Symbolism of Reason, Rite and Art*, by Susanne Langer. Mrs Langer was a distinguished twentieth century American philosopher whose work is very much in the European tradition. I realized as I began to read her book that she was closely familiar with all the works of all the philosophers I had ever heard of, and of scores more that I hadn't. But this was in no way a book that merely played around with strange ideas, or presented a brilliant analysis of something no ordinary human being would care twopence about.

Langer's concern was to explain the very ways we think and feel, and represent our thoughts and feelings to ourselves. Since language is the most powerful medium we use to articulate our thoughts, an analysis of how language must have come about and developed is central to her critique. And all I could find myself saying, as I followed her, spellbound, from page to page, was "Yes, she is right, this must have been so. This *must* have been so."

She was examining the kind of language which was an intimate part of my daily existence. She talked about the growth of language in a childhood I could recognize: a childhood where, for instance, chairs looked stern, or dignified. (I remember that my sister and I called chairs in the dining room with backs ending in points 'witch' chairs, while others with more rounded, flowing lines were 'princess' ones.)

For the human mind, Langer declared, saw reality symbolically. Rather than being a transmitter, it was more like a great transformer. From all the sheer shrieking mass of sense data surrounding us, our sense organs select predominant forms which become meanings. And we can commandeer practically anything – any arbitrary sounds, shapes, sensations – to stand as symbols for those meanings, and so bring them into our minds. The new key to an understanding of the human mind lay in recognizing that at the root of our entire mental life is the power of abstractive seeing, and of symbolization. (Langer defines a symbol, with crystal elegance, as 'any device whereby we are enabled to make an abstraction'.)

I still find it difficult to overrate the importance of this insight. Far too many students of linguistics, it seems to me, have been sidetracked by their concern with the outward forms of language, with the way we arrange words, how we hear or see them, how we learn them, and how we use them. Whole books have been expended on such topics, and yet nothing very much seems to have been said when the last page is reached; we are none the wiser for having tried to follow their often tortuous arguments. Langer's work makes clear that what is wrong with such investigations is just that they are starting in the wrong place. For it is not the use of words which lies at the heart of language, but the *construction of meaning*.

Once we have grasped this idea, everything else falls into place around it. Some years later, when I was trying to help my daughters learn maths more confidently than had ever been possible for me, I stumbled over Seton Pollock's *The Basic Colour Factor Guide*. I read it with the same mounting sense of excitement and recognition that had marked my exploration of Susanne Langer's work.

Pollock developed the Colour Factor Set – a collection of coloured blocks very like the Cuisenaire rods, but with much more emphasis on the factor structure of numbers. If you multiply 2 x 3 you get 6 – do it with the Colour Factor blocks and you multiply a pink block by a light blue one, matching a violet block. Soon you can look at the '12' block, which is mauve, and 'see' all its factors – 2 (pink), another 2 giving a deeper pink, and 3 (light blue). Or you can replace 2 x 3 with two violet blocks – violet multiplied by pink still gives you the same mauve.

Ideas like prime numbers, and powers of numbers (2 x 2 x 2, or 2^3), can be made immediately visible with these blocks – very young children can discover the first few prime numbers for themselves, by trying to construct factor lines for 2, 3, 5, 7 and 11. The only lines that will fit these numbers exactly are rows of ones. (So the definition of a prime number becomes obvious, almost tangible – any number whose only factors are itself and one.)

It was Pollock who pointed out that learning common nouns involves appreciating the highest common factors and lowest common multiples of sets of ideas, also that the conception of ratio is essential to virtually all our thinking processes. Armed with these two insights, I could then see how the other mathematical procedures were also part and parcel of language learning, and of our basic, overwhelming determination to fashion meaning from experience.

Discovering the little red book

The third book found me between Susanne Langer and *The Basic Colour Factor Guide*, and for all practical purposes was the most important. I was in a book shop at the time, having arranged to meet my husband there later in the afternoon, but I had arrived about forty minutes early.

My attention was caught by a book on display on the other side of the room, large white lettering on a red cover, declaring boldly *Teach Your Baby to Read*.

As a fairly recent college graduate, my first reaction was one of instant disdain. Clearly the author, Glenn Doman, hadn't done my college education courses, and was not aware of the damage that could result from teaching children to read before they were 'ready'. Surely he couldn't be serious, he couldn't mean real babies. Or if he did mean real babies, then what he had in mind was not real reading. But since I had time to spare, (and after all I did have two small children at home), I might as well investigate and see what nonsense he was talking. From these lofty heights, I picked up the book.

I stood transfixed, hardly aware of turning the pages, devouring the print. I had the sense of curtain after curtain falling away, and all that was revealed behind them clear and transparent. "Why did no one else ever explain reading like this?" I kept saying to myself. "This will change everything." Dream-like, I bought the book, and when Glyn appeared was standing quiet and shiny-eyed, clutching my new possession.

Doman worked with brain-damaged children in Philadelphia, and discovered that it was possible to teach them to read at very early ages: three, two or younger. Doman showed the parents how to do it, and the parents did the teaching. After a while the parents protested that what was happening was unfair. Why should their brain-damaged youngsters have so many advantages, when normal children, in ordinary (American) schools, didn't begin learning to read until they were six? Doman registered these concerns, and so wrote his book for the parents of all children, brain-damaged or not.

What excited me about my find, though, was not so much the revelation that babies could literally engage in real reading. No, I was glued to the spot by Doman's explanation of *why* this was possible.

He is saying something very simple (one reason we overlooked it for so long). Doman points out that a spoken word is a pattern of sounds, it registers in a baby's mind by way of his ears, and the baby learns to understand it – that is, to associate it with an idea. So far, so good. We all know that.

But then Doman goes on to point out that a written word is a pattern of shapes. It registers in a baby's mind by way of his eyes, and the baby learns to understand it in just the same way as a spoken word – by associating it with an idea.

In other words, the process of understanding print is very closely comparable to the process of understanding speech: reading is like hearing, which is why babies can do it...

I should have known. Of course he was right, he had to be right. The comparison fitted in most beautifully with Langer's ideas about the workings of language – that we can use *any* kind of sense data to represent concepts. Sounds, or shapes, it makes no odds; just so long as they are readily perceptible, and can be combined and recombined in an infinite number of different patterns. Because what matters is not the sounds as such, or the shapes as such; *but the ideas which they represent.*

If children can use patterns of sounds to help them perform all the amazing intellectual feats described in the last chapter, why shouldn't they be able to use patterns of shapes in the same way? There is no essential difference between the two forms, which makes shapes harder to perceive than sounds. It is as easy to distinguish shapes, and see them in patterns, as it is to make out sounds, and hear them in patterns.

Now Doman was affirming that there was indeed no difference in the ways the two forms of language were understood. If babies were exposed to meaningful written language, as helpfully and as abundantly as they were exposed to speech, they would learn to understand it just as well.

All children could do it, whether they were deaf, blind (they could feel the shapes), brain damaged, or apparently 'normal'. They could do it at five, four, three or two years of age – the younger the better: Doman has found that children can learn to read more easily at four than at five, more easily at three than at four, more easily at two than at three. Two is probably the ideal age to begin reading, because it is the optimum age for learning language in any form.

Most two year olds don't learn to read, not because they can't, but because it doesn't occur to most parents to surround them with large, clear, plainly visible written language. But when we take the trouble to do this, and keep on pointing out the words, telling our children what they mean and what they say, even toddlers can learn to read them.

Learning print like speech

I had to explore Doman's ideas for myself, I realized. But from the outset, I was not trying to find out if it was possible to teach babies to read – Doman had proved that beyond doubt, as far as I was concerned.

The question burning in my mind was a different one. Could Doman be right about written language? Was it really understood like speech? If so, what were the implications for our teaching methods, both at home and at school – for the ways in which we helped children to experience and understand print?

This is why it is so necessary to begin with an examination of how children do learn to understand speech. And the operative word in that sentence is 'learn', because spoken language is most definitely learned: which means that it has to be taught, even if we are hardly aware of ourselves as teaching it. So what do we do (or, more importantly, what *don't* we do) when we are helping babies learn to understand the language that they hear?

For a start, we don't assume that learning to hear language is an advanced intellectual process which should not be undertaken before the age of five.

We do not say that only professionals should teach children to hear. (Thank goodness we don't: there aren't enough professionals to go around.)

We don't say to a baby, "I am not going to introduce any new words today, until you have proved to me that you have learned all the new words I said yesterday."

We are not continually testing and assessing babies to find out how well they are learning: we don't think about their progress in those terms.

We don't say that only one person should teach a baby to hear, and if he hears lots of people talking, he will become very confused.

We don't feel that spoken language should be doled out to the baby in coffee spoons, in tiny and carefully graduated amounts. Quite the reverse, we know that the more spoken language he hears, the more he will learn to understand, and the more easily he will understand it.

Unfortunately, we do do most or all of these things, with the best of intentions, when children are learning to read. It is only as we make the direct comparison with how they learn to hear language, that we realize it is probably our very assumptions about the reading process which are causing the damage, and erecting quite needless stumbling blocks in the children's way.

How can we remove these stumbling blocks?

Doman begins with single words, in fact he begins with names, which makes complete sense when we acknowledge that that is how babies begin learning to hear. (From now on, I shall use the expression 'learning to hear' as shorthand for 'learning to hear language', just to save time and space.) Babies are not concerned with whole sentences at first, they are far too busy registering labels for all the people and objects in their experience, as I described in Chapter II.

Now if he is going to learn a particular spoken word, a child has to be able to recognize it: *he must know that he has heard it before.* So there must be a recording of the word stored in his head, which works like a sort of template. Whenever he hears that same word in the future, it matches with the 'template', and the baby recognizes it straightaway. Because this recording, or template, is already closely associated with a meaning, the child invests the heard word with the very same meaning; so he recognizes the word, and understands it, in an instant. For example, he hears the word 'chair', matches it with his own previous 'recording' of the word, and understands immediately what is meant. (If we didn't do this, we would never be able to recognize words at all.)

In order to form a nice clear recording of a word, a child must hear it clearly in the first place. This is why we say words slowly and precisely when we are helping children to learn them. When Gwynneth was going round and round her grandparents' kitchen, demanding names for everything she could see, I instinctively pronounced each label very carefully – 'sink', 'bowl', 'chair', 'cupboard', 'stove', because I could feel that this was what was needed. The meaning of each word was right there in front of her, so template and meaning registered in her mind at the same moment.

Doman applies the same principles to his early reading vocabularies. The words are large, in thick red letters, which makes it very easy for a small child to form clear mental images of the words, and so recognize them with no trouble.

I promptly set about using Doman's big red words with my two 'babies' – Helen aged three, and Gwynneth aged two. In no time at all they were learning ten new words every day, reading them in sentences and in books, and looking round for more.

That experience more than anything convinced me Doman was right about the workings of written language. The speed and ease with which both little girls learned to read had everything to do, I felt sure, with the fact that they were experiencing print like speech. It is much too vague to describe what I was doing as a conventional 'whole word' approach. It was the *way* I presented the words that mattered. The words were always big and easy to see, reducing in size only gradually, so the children could form really clear mental images. We moved on to storybooks as soon as possible. Most crucial of all, I concentrated on teaching, not testing, forever indicating the words and providing their meanings, gently correcting the children when they stumbled. 'Failure' did not exist. Helen and Gwynneth couldn't help but learn the words and sentences, just as they couldn't help but learn to understand the language they were hearing.

What about phonics?

Doman maintains that it isn't necessary to teach phonics, and you can see what he means. You don't have to know phonics in order to understand spoken words; so if you understand written words like spoken words, then you don't need phonics in order to read.

But something wasn't right. I knew that I still 'sounded out' words in my head, even at my advanced age – the procedure hadn't been jettisoned along with congruent triangles and Latin declensions, as soon as I left school. So it must be a useful thing to do; and I wanted my children to be able to do everything with written words that I could.

Teaching the procedure

I decided to teach phonics as a separate process, alongside the process of understanding print, but just as fast. We started on the alphabet when the children had reading vocabularies of about 70 words. Then, because they were so little, and I couldn't expect them to work out the technique for themselves, I simply demonstrated how to match sounds to letters, using the 'tallying' procedure which a Scottish primary school was later to take on board with spectacular effect. "That word says 'pond', doesn't it. Now, if we cover all the letters except 'p', it says 'pŭ'. Now it says 'pŏ'," [uncovering the 'o'] "now it says 'pon' – and now, hey presto, it says 'pond' again! You do it." So they did; and went on like this, with my encouragement, until they were spontaneously sounding out all their new words, before reading them.

We finished the alphabet in one and a half months; two-letter sounds in another month; and the 'magic' letters 'e', 'i' and 'y' in about another month. So three and a half months after I began teaching the alphabet, my daughters could sound out any words they came across, including 'irregular' words; and they could read anything at their interest level, independently, fluently and accurately.

They also taught themselves to write, by copying words on the blackboard, which I had craftily painted in their room.

They were both fully literate in less than a year: my younger daughter before she was even three years old.

I was as surprised as anybody. Although Doman's comparison between print and speech had struck home straightaway, I was, even so, amazed to see his ideas borne out in practice: that when you presented written language as fast and as helpfully as spoken language, tiny children could indeed learn to read.

The purpose of phonics

I still couldn't understand how phonics fitted in to the analogy. I knew it was different from understanding print, and I knew it was necessary – but exactly why and how?

Doman suggests that if parents spoke only in whispers, but their words were flashed onto nearby walls while they spoke, in big bold letters, their children would grow up understanding written language, but not speech. I decided to pursue the idea, and invented a little boy called Wayne, who learned to read in this very way. When he was five, he went to school – and his teachers embarked on the difficult and time-consuming task of teaching him to understand *spoken* language.

They had a choice of methods. They could use the 'whole word' or 'hear-and-see' approach, which worked pretty well, but meant that someone always had to be on hand to show Wayne the written words that matched his new spoken words. Or, because spoken words were made of sounds, which more or less matched the separate letters in written words, they could teach Wayne to visualize the appropriate written words in response to spoken words, independently – by mapping letters onto sounds. This was a much better plan, because it meant that Wayne could teach himself to understand new spoken words, by matching them with meaningful print.

At this point, I became quite elated. Doman was right, as far as he went. Babies who could only hear didn't need to know phonics; and babies who could only read didn't need phonics either. But phonics was necessary when *a second form of language was introduced* – and it became useful for children not only to understand both forms, but also to match them with each other. Children who could do this by themselves, fitting the words together bit by bit, obviously had a great advantage over children who couldn't – because they could teach themselves to understand the unfamiliar form, by matching it with the familiar one.

The transfer of meaning can work in either direction.

By the time most children start learning to read, in school, they are already past masters of spoken language. So it makes sense to use speech to help make the new form of language meaningful to them.

If we wanted to, we could build up meanings for print by direct reference to the same kind of physical contexts which first provided the meanings for speech. E.g. we could put written labels on all the objects in the classroom, we could hold up written sentences describing different activities engaged in by the children (and some of this sort of thing is no bad plan).

But why on earth rely on such an approach when the children have spent the first few years of their lives constructing meanings and learning to represent those meanings in words? Let's capitalize on their existing knowledge of language to help them see the same meanings in written words. If we point to the word 'frog', and tell a child, "That word says 'frog'," he can transfer the meaning from the spoken word, which he already understands, to the written word. A picture of a frog would be nice, but it isn't essential: the child has a perfectly good mental picture of a frog whenever he hears the spoken word.

When we point to the written sentence 'Sarah is climbing a tree,' and say it aloud, the child imagines what Sarah is doing in response to the spoken sentence, and begins to see those very same meanings in the written words.

The only drawback is that we have to keep on telling the children what written words say all the time. If we could teach them to match written words with spoken words *by themselves*, they could transfer meanings from speech to print *by themselves*, and therefore teach themselves to understand the written words...

So phonics is a brilliant short cut. It enables children to use all the resources of their spoken language in order to learn to read, and that has to be a good idea.

But the tide of meaning can also flow from print to speech. This is because it is quite possible to learn the meanings of many words by reading them first.

For example, Helen informed her father one day that she didn't think he would look very nice with a 'mowst-ake' – and was most put out to be met with blank incomprehension. She had to explain she was talking about the bristly bits along a man's top lip, then we understood. "Oh Helen, you mean a moustache!"

Never in any language had Helen heard the word 'mowst-ake', which was original with her, but she knew perfectly well what it meant. So she must have learned the meaning of the word by reading it – saying it aloud was a different process, not necessary to her understanding.

Most children who spend a fair amount of time reading learn the meanings of scores of words in this way. If they have also learned phonics they can say them aloud as well. Usually they will pronounce the words correctly, but their mispronunciations should alert us to the process which is actually taking place. I remember talking about 'stiffling' heat when I was little, or children being terribly 'dick-ent' (decent) to each other. (You can tell I was brought up on Enid Blyton.)

In this instance, phonics is not helping children to read, it is helping them to speak! Matching the written words with spoken words enables them to supply their speaking vocabularies with all the words they are learning to understand by reading them: and in the long run, this will be even more useful than transferring meanings from speech to print.

Learning to read aloud is like learning to speak

It suddenly dawned on me that mapping uttered words onto written words, bit by bit (phonics), was *exactly* like learning to speak. A baby learning to pronounce a new spoken word correctly is mapping his feelings of utterance, bit by bit, onto the pattern of sounds coming into his ears. (See Chapter II.) A child learning to sound out a written word is mapping his feelings of utterance, bit by bit, onto the pattern of shapes in front of him. The procedure is the same, and the purpose is the same as well – transferring meanings from one form of language (heard sounds, visual shapes, vocal sensations) to another.

So understanding print is just like understanding speech. Learning to read aloud is just like learning to speak. The analogy between written language and spoken language holds good all the way along the line, and written language really is a sort of looking glass world for spoken language.

Each world can function in its own way and on its own terms, but there is a direct connection between them which enables us to step from one world to the other whenever we choose. That connection is phonics.

IV

Explaining dyslexia

The literacy strugglers

I was so enchanted by the looking glass world I had stumbled upon, and seeing how phonics fitted in to the picture, that I had to write about it.

I described my journey of discovery, and Helen and Gwynneth learning to read and write, in my first book, which I called *The Real Reading Revolution*. I sent off the typescript to Doman's UK publishers, Jonathan Cape.

They liked it, and agreed to take the project on board – but they didn't like the title. It had to be altered to *Reading and Writing Before School*, otherwise the book wouldn't be nearly so marketable.

This was quite a disappointment for me. To my mind, it was the analogy between written language and spoken language which was of paramount importance, and would bring about the 'real revolution' in our thinking. It had implications for the teaching of literacy everywhere, to all children, at home or at school, whatever their age, and whatever their handicaps might be. It didn't really matter how old children were when you began teaching them to read, so long as you concentrated, with all your might and main, on teaching print like speech. Working with preschool children was exciting, for parents who wanted to do it, but it wasn't the most significant aspect of the whole thing, by any means. In itself, it merely helped to demonstrate the truth of the analogy between written language and spoken language. I wanted teachers, teacher trainers, educationists and child psychologists to read my book, as well as parents, but that was unlikely to happen with the change of title.

However, Cape were adamant, and I felt I had no choice but to agree. So *Reading and Writing Before School* (written when my name was Felicity Hughes) was published in 1971. There were American, German and Italian editions, as well as a paperback one after a couple of years, but eventually the book sank into oblivion and disappeared.

Meanwhile we had come home to England again. Partly on the strength of my published work, as well as my teaching qualifications, I was given a job as Literacy Support teacher at a small secondary school in Devon. I have always liked the 11-14 age group, when children are just beginning to spread their wings and fly into adulthood, but still have all the options open to them, they haven't yet made irrevocable choices. I was very keen to follow up my ideas about literacy, and find out if it was possible to teach reading and writing as naturally in a school as I had done at home, but primary school teaching has never appealed to me. So, inevitably, at secondary level, I found myself working with the literacy strugglers.

I didn't understand, at first, why they were having problems. Many of them were highly articulate, and could talk the hind leg off a donkey, so why did they fall apart when faced with a page of print? I was utterly convinced that written language did indeed work just like spoken language, and this indicated they had the mental processes necessary for reading and writing. Maybe they had never been helped to experience written language in the right way.

I was aware of the term 'dyslexia', but all I knew about it at that time was that the dictionary defined it as 'word blindness' – which made no sense at all. How was it that children who could see everything else in their environment perfectly well (chairs, tables, doors, blackboards, each other) suddenly lost the power of vision when it came to black squiggles on white paper, which essentially were no different from the chairs, tables, doors, etc.?

I didn't worry about it at first; and anyway the l.e.a. frowned upon the term 'dyslexia', insisting that we should talk about a 'specific learning difficulty' instead. That was merely stating the obvious, I felt; it contributed nothing towards any genuine understanding of the condition.

Simon's story

But after a parents' evening for the new entrants, I was tackled by a worried Head of the Lower School. Simon's mother had bent his ear for some considerable time at the meeting, demanding to know if we were aware that her son was dyslexic, and what were we doing about it?

It was news to me, as Simon had not been placed in any of my remedial groups. I informed the Head that we could answer the questions he had been asked very easily: we had no idea that Simon was dyslexic, so we weren't doing a blessed thing about it.

This was probably massaged slightly in the translation back to Simon's mum, to the effect that we knew about Simon's problems, and all possible steps were being taken, etc. etc. But Simon's mother was not to be fooled, and kept complaining about our inaction to anyone who would listen. In desperation the Head told me we had to do *something*.

There were one or two lessons on my timetable allocated for individual work, so I borrowed Simon and gave him a word recognition test, reasoning that if he was 'word blind' he must have reading problems. But to my surprise Simon did pretty well on the test, with a reading age only a year and a half behind his chronological age – not brilliant, but perfectly adequate for his classroom tasks. "I don't understand this, Simon," I said in genuine puzzlement. "How can you be dyslexic if you can read?"

And Simon said (I had no inkling then how significant his answer was going to be) – Simon said, "It's not my reading so much, Miss, *it's my spelling.*"

The Schonell spelling test more than confirmed Simon's diagnosis – he had a spelling age of only six and a half, four *years* behind his reading age, five and a half behind his actual age!

Now I was completely baffled. As far as I was concerned, accurate spelling was a matter of looking at the mental images of words, and copying them onto the page. Simon couldn't do this, so presumably the correct images weren't there in his head. On the other hand, his reading age seemed to indicate that the matching images *were* there in his head, else how could he have recognized the words on the test paper?

I had to find some kind of explanation, but ruled out virtually all the standard reasons for literacy difficulties before I started on my quest. I knew that the acquisition of spoken language was a highly intelligent process, so the cause of dyslexia could not be a lack of intelligence or ability. Nor could the literacy strugglers be poor learners, since spoken language was the product of sheer learning. Then, spoken words and sentences were particular sequences of sounds, so children who could manipulate sounds adroitly couldn't be bad at sequencing as such, either.

It began to look as if the Oxford Dictionary had to be right in its definition of dyslexia as 'word blindness', and the cause must be some kind of perceptual disorder – but what and how, and why the huge discrepancy between Simon's reading level and his spelling?

Orton's explanation

To my surprise I found what I was looking for quite speedily, in Samuel Torrey Orton's *Reading, Writing and Speech Problems in Children*, published as long ago as 1937, by W. W. Norton. Orton points out that the brain is divided into two hemispheres, and the left side of the brain is the 'language centre', where most words are recorded. But certain aspects of language are recorded in the right hemisphere, and when this happens with written words, they are the mirror image of their counterparts registered on the left.

Most children succeed in blocking out the images, or 'engrams', that are recorded on the right side of the brain, when they are learning to read and write. But some children don't. So sometimes they visualize a word the right way round. Sometimes they visualize the mirror image. And sometimes the two images merge and overlap, so they visualize bits of the word the right way round, while one end snakes back on itself, and turns up in the middle, back to front. Or it rolls itself over, from top to bottom. Or it can do both at the same time, neatly transposing 'p's into 'd's, 'y's into 'h's, 'm's into 'w's.

This means that the word 'apple', for instance, could appear in the child's head in different forms at different times. It could be 'seen' as 'alepp', or 'pelap', or 'abble', or 'plead' – or 'apple', but the child has no way of knowing that that is the correct version, they are all equally correct to him.

Children who copy these jumbles, faithfully, produce the bizarre spelling which baffles so many English teachers trying to mark their work. (It not only baffles teachers, it baffles parents, friends, and usually the children themselves, when they come to re-read what they have written, even just a short time later.):

The jumbles give rise to reading problems too, because the child has great difficulty in recognizing the words on the page. The words in his head may match up with the words he sees, or they may not – so he may seem to 'know' a word one day, but the next day he doesn't. This, then, explains why dyslexia has been called 'word blindness' – but the word on the page behaves itself beautifully; it's the word in the child's head which is playing tricks. So he can see the words in front of him perfectly well, he just can't recognize them.

If someone has read to him a great deal, though, while he follows the print, he gradually forms mental clusters of words (like 'alepp', 'pelap', 'abble' etc.), which all mean the same thing. Now when he sees the word 'apple', it matches with this mental cluster, so he does recognize it – although he still can't spell it.

Simon's mother had indeed read to him a great deal when he was younger, which explained why his reading was fairly good, but his spelling was hopeless.

Orton calls the condition 'strephosymbolia', or 'twisted symbols' – an illuminating definition. He also indicates that it is much more frequent in boys than in girls. Miles (see below) reports the same imbalance, with a ratio of about 4¼ males to 1 female.

The Bangor Dyslexia Test

I was thrilled by my discovery of Orton's work, because it fitted in so beautifully to the jigsaw puzzle taking shape in front of me. It meant that dyslexia was basically a perceptual problem, not one of ability. It is caused by a confusion of the images recorded in both hemispheres of the brain, and gives rise to difficulty in other areas besides reading and writing. Children with literacy problems frequently have trouble distinguishing between left and right; they muddle up the alphabet, days of the week and months of the year; they can't tell the time on analogue clocks; numbers have a nasty habit of reversing themselves, and multiplication tables may be a complete minefield.

When you think about it, most of us form visual images of these things. I can 'see' the alphabet, mentally, running from left to right across my mind, and if I focus on a particular letter, e.g. 'n', I can 'see' it coming after 'm' and before 'o'. Days of the week and months of the year go from right to left, for some reason, but once again I can 'see' their relative positions quite easily. I picture the time on a clock face as soon as someone mentions it. And multiplication tables form little blocks in my head, with the answers neatly listed down the right hand side!

If these visual images are getting muddled up for some children, or perhaps are never there at all, it is not surprising that the youngsters find it hard going to recall such items in the proper order.

So a test for dyslexia needs to focus on this left-right confusion (rather than reading age, spelling age, or IQ levels). The *Bangor Dyslexia Test*, developed by T. R. Miles, does exactly that. (See his book *Dyslexia: The Pattern of Difficulties*.) It begins by asking a child to perform certain actions, for instance 'point to my right ear with your left hand', and includes reciting some multiplication tables, plus saying the months forwards – and backwards. It also records b-d confusion (a classic for dyslexic children). The test has been validated by comparing the results for children who suffer from literacy difficulties and those who don't: it therefore gives us a pretty accurate indication of whether dyslexia exists or not.

(However, I am increasingly wary of relying on such diagnostic tests before taking action. I now feel it is much more positive to teach all children, right from the start, as if any single child could be dyslexic – see my final chapter.)

The bright side of the spelling problem

Meanwhile, at secondary level, I was continuing with my efforts to teach like a parent, rather than like a teacher. I fitted out my room with a carpet and easy chairs, and splurged on as many delectable books as I could find that had matching word-for-word tapes. "Here's a cassette player and some headphones," I would say to a youngster. "Choose any book you want, plus the tape – the deal is that at some point I want you to follow the print while you listen to the tape. It's quite easy when you get going. If you decide you don't like a particular book after a couple of chapters, for heaven's sake pack it in and choose another one. I want you to enjoy what you're reading – that's all."

They were hesitant at first, hardly daring to believe that I meant what I said, and they really could choose any book from the enticing display on the shelves, just like their peers in mainstream lessons. Didn't I know they couldn't read? But soon, cocooned in headphones, and turning the pages with gathering confidence, they found that they *could* read, there was nothing to it after all. The odd chuckle and exclamation of delight were more than enough confirmation for me that I was on the right lines, and very often they would insist on telling me about what they had read at the end of the lesson. "Go on with it at home," I would say, "read the best bits to Mum and Dad – I bet you can."

A great advantage enjoyed by parents is that they can teach their children individually, one-to-one. (I had done this with Helen and Gwynneth.) It might seem virtually impossible to achieve such a desirable state of affairs in a school setting, but I did my best, extracting three or four children at a time from their mainstream classes, and roping in volunteers to provide extra tuition. One child listening to tapes, book in hand; one on a computer; one with a volunteer, and one with me. At half time we all moved round! We were making progress, I thought: slow progress, but we were moving forward nevertheless.

Then I had the bright idea of inviting parents in to an after school literacy club, when they would work with their own child, under my guidance. (This meant that they could continue practising at home, which would make a real difference.) I stressed that the parents had far more knowledge of their child than I did, and I wanted to learn from them as well as vice versa. I knew how much I didn't know about dyslexia, but I was determined to go on finding out.

The parents were touchingly grateful to discover a teacher who was open minded on the subject, and willing to defer to their experience. They began treating me like a human being, instead of like an 'authority'. Ashley's mother rang up one evening. (Ashley's writing was indecipherable, but he could design computer programmes as if he were composing a symphony.) "Felicity," she said excitedly, "did you watch *Horizon*?" Curses, curses, no I hadn't. What was it about? "Well, it was about dyslexia, and it was so positive – it was about all the things dyslexics are good at, for a change. Did you know that many great architects are dyslexic? And sculptors? And chess players? And computer programmers?! Ashley sat watching it like a cat that has swallowed the cream. It did him the world of good."

This was fascinating. All my students were brilliant, I was convinced of that, but why architecture, particularly? Why sculpture, and chess? What was the common theme, the connecting link – or was it just coincidence? Orton's work had made clear that literacy problems often resulted from a confusion of the images perceived in both hemispheres of the brain. Could it be that something which was such a liability in one respect was an asset in others? Time to sit down and ponder.

I pondered. It was when two images merged and overlapped that written words went haywire. But it's when two images merge that we see 'in the round', stereoscopically. I harked back to the intriguing picture books of my childhood, printed in red and green. You looked at them through coloured plastic lenses, and the images leapt from the page. Without the lenses, they were flat and double edged again. Was it possible that dyslexics were visualizing *in three dimensions?* And not just written words, but space and form? That would explain the gift for architecture, sculpture, drawing and painting, electronics, chess. Einstein and Churchill, I knew, were said to have been dyslexic. And Einstein visualized reality not just in two dimensions, not just in three, but in four at least, and possibly in many more. Churchill could review every theatre of the second world war in a single mental glance...

A new world opened in front of me. I began to look at what my students were doing, all over again. Here was a child with mirror image spelling and chaotic handwriting. The received wisdom was that he lacked the necessary co-ordination and motor skills to form his letters properly. *So how could the same child move his pencil so fluently over the page when it came to drawing?* And here was another, and another. Edward floundered desperately when he tried to write, but felt tip painting was a different matter. Blocks of shape and colour that balanced in perfect harmony, instinctively arranged with an artist's eye, and pen.

Lee's spelling was the bane of his life. Fortunately he too watched the *Horizon* programme that I missed: with a lengthening smile, and then he went to fetch his mother. "You must watch this, Mum," he instructed gently, sitting her down in front of the screen. "It's about me." Lee did the 'impossible' drawings – the blocks of wood that go in opposite directions depending on which way you look at them. Or he spent hours drawing patterns of cubes that recede one minute, stand out the next, as your perception shifts. His favourite subject, however, was dinosaurs. What Lee didn't know about dinosaurs was not worth knowing, and he could classify them minutely, down to the last wrinkle of skin or menacing claw. Lee and I did a *Headwork* exercise together which involved identifying insects by means of a flow chart. He didn't enthuse particularly, he felt it should have been about dinosaurs. Since he could find nothing along those lines in any of the *Headwork* books, the following week he brought in the exercise he would like to have done:

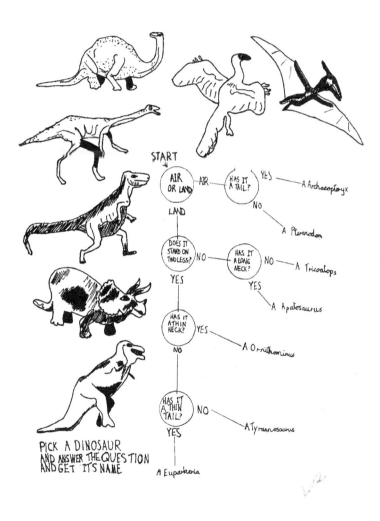

START

AIR OR LAND — AIR — HAS IT A TAIL? — YES — A Archaeopteryx

NO — A Pteranodon

LAND

DOES IT STAND ON TWO LEGS? — NO — HAS IT A LONG NECK? — NO — A Tricoatops

YES — A Apatosaurus

YES

HAS IT A THIN NECK? — YES — A Ornithominus

NO

HAS IT A THIN TAIL? — NO — A Tyrannosaurus

YES

A Euparkeria

PICK A DINOSAUR AND ANSWER THE QUESTION AND GET ITS NAME

I studied his work, absorbed. The theme was now becoming familiar: not only the skill in drawing, but also the feeling for shape and pattern and logical progression. "Lee, this is beautiful, can I put it in my book? And can I put the cube one in as well?" "Oh yes, Miss, if you want." He placed his compositions, with loving care, on a high shelf, for me to find when I needed them.

'They cannot concentrate, these children,' is more received wisdom; and it is true that some days, when you are working with them, what you say doesn't seem to register because they are elsewhere, marching to a different drum. (Other days they come storming back, and bowl you over with the insights they have garnered on their travels.)

But concentration? I went round to have a chat with Ben's mum, and while we talked, eleven-year-old Ben was stretched full length on the floor, working on his picture of a goose. For an hour and a half he concentrated, oblivious to everything around him, now and then going to fetch a tin of white enamel, or gold for the eggs. He cleaned his brush carefully between the colours.

At last he sat back on his heels and looked at what he had done. He returned to the world of people. "Do you like it, Miss?" "Yes I do, Ben, very much. I don't suppose you would bring it in to school, and let me put it on the wall?" "If you want, Miss, I'll bring it in tomorrow, when it's dry."

So then, when I was tempted to bewail any child's lack of concentration, I had Ben's goose to remind me.

Ben

I began to tell other parents about what was happening, so they too could discover the bright side of their special children. Avadne, like me, found it an eye opener. The previous year she and I had worked with Darren, a Year 10 student, who had grown very demoralized because of his spelling. (He perked up when I told him he was in illustrious company, and kept mentioning Einstein and Churchill at strategic intervals.) He swooshed through a diagnostic dictation, working out most of the spelling cues himself (see Chapter V), and began to think he was someone who could, rather than someone who couldn't. Class teachers remarked that he was now writing with confidence, and at length, and his spelling had improved dramatically. What was happening? Ask his mum, I said smugly, ask Avadne, she's the one who's done it. Now Avadne thought back to Darren's earlier years. "He loved Lego, and meccano, and things like that. And I tell you what, Felicity, we could never understand it – he used to do jigsaw puzzles for fun, with the *reverse side uppermost!* I didn't think of connecting that with his wonky spelling, though."

Of course she didn't, not with just the one child. No more did I, with any number of students. But now, thanks to a *Horizon* programme I didn't see, and parents who wanted to help, I had learned that these talents and skills were most assuredly 'part of the territory', and all we had to do was look out for them, and *point them out to the child.* Often he didn't know they were there either, he was so used to thinking of himself as someone of no account, just a struggler. He needed to know, he needed to be told.

My daughter Gwynneth, grown up and an artist herself, a telephone call away, was intrigued by what she called 'Mum's passion'. I nattered to her at length on the phone, and she could see what I couldn't. I told her about Jonathan's snake. The head glared fiercely, hanging from the top of the page, fangs poised to strike. At the bottom of the page the tip of the snake's tail appeared. "Isn't that lovely," I said, "the rest of the snake isn't there at all, it exists only in his imagination." "Oh mother," declared Gwynneth patiently, "don't you know where the rest of the snake is? It's on the other side of the page, of course!" Of course.

Another time the phone jangled again. "Mother, you must watch the Q.E.D. programme in fifteen minutes, it's right up your street." I watched obediently (I was going to anyway). 'The Foolish Wise Ones' – les idiots savants. Three people forcing their way through one tiny chink in the barriers hedged around them, all with unbelievable gifts. The third brought me to the edge of my seat. He was a severely limited autistic child, but he could draw any of London's buildings from memory, in perfect perspective. (See Stephen Wiltshire, *Drawings*.) A fellow practitioner said that he was probably the most brilliant child artist living in Britain. "Look at that – most artists have to convey perspective by means of shading. Stephen does it all with lines, it's amazing." I felt my spine tingle, thinking dyslexia. Would there be any indication? Nobody had mentioned literacy. He was taken to St Pancras' Station, which he had never seen before, and allowed to study it for fifteen minutes. Later, his drawing emerged, shape, form, detail, depth, solidity, flowing across the page. The only thing wrong with it, said the presenters, baffled, was that he had drawn it *the wrong way round*.

I leapt back to the phone. "Gwynneth, did you see, he drew St Pancras' Station the wrong way round!" "I know, I know, Mum, isn't it exciting!"

Of course he drew St Pancras' Station the wrong way round. And I would lay any money he cannot spell to save his soul.

Ron Davis and The Gift of Dyslexia

Some years later another book appeared over the horizon: Ron Davis' *The Gift of Dyslexia*. Ron Davis is himself dyslexic, and describes the ability to visualize in three dimensions from his own first hand experience. Because his background is not the same as mine, he explains the phenomenon rather differently, but there are so many parallels between what he is saying, and the independent conclusions I had reached, that I felt his book offered real confirmation of Orton's analysis.

Suppose a youngster has developed the ability to 'see' all the way round objects, at a very early age. He notices a paw sticking out from under a chair, and immediately pictures a whole cat on the other side of the paw. In this instance, his visualizing gift resolves any confusion he might have had about the creature, so is clearly a good thing. He uses it again and again, and it always works.

That is, until he starts school, and is expected to get to grips with written words. Most children find their initial encounters with print confusing, when someone is expecting them to work out, unaided, what the words mean and say. However, our young dyslexic has a well-honed technique for resolving confusion: he promptly tries to *see all the way round the words* – but instead of resolving the confusion, this makes it far worse. Not realizing what has happened, the child goes on using his old method, for tackling new confusions; and digs himself deeper and deeper into a pit of frustration and failure.

But Davis' book is a triumph of optimism, not despair. He declares that dyslexia is indeed a gift, characterized by great intuition, imagination and creativity. He describes how dyslexics can defeat their confusion and take charge of their own mental processes; and not only learn to read and write as well as anybody else, but also enrich the world with their own unique talents.

Scotopic Sensitivity (Irlen) Syndrome

In the latter half of the twentieth century, an American school psychologist, Helen Irlen, became increasingly frustrated by the failure of the educational system to help children with literacy problems. Some youngsters had particular difficulty reading black print on white paper. After years of research, she discovered that many strugglers experienced a dramatic improvement in their ability to read when transparent coloured overlays were placed over the page. Glasses with coloured lenses helped even more, in more areas: copying text from a blackboard or overhead projector, using computers, and writing.

She realized that the children were suffering from a particular perceptual disorder which she named Scotopic Sensitivity Syndrome, or SSS – but in deference to her work it is now termed Scotopic Sensitivity (Irlen) Syndrome.

Irlen has never been able to pinpoint exactly why the coloured overlays/lenses make such a difference, but one explanation she has offered is that the separate colours combined in black print register in the brain at different speeds. This causes blurred, shaky, swirling or moving images of written words. (See Helen Irlen, *Reading by the Colors*, Avery Publishing Group, 1991.) The coloured overlays or glasses filter out the colours coming in at the wrong speed. Result: the perceived words are nice and clear, stop jumping about, and are much more comfortable to read.

Whatever the explanation, there is so much evidence that coloured filters can literally transform a child's outlook on life, that it makes sense to offer overlays or glasses to every child who needs them. Irlen Syndrome can affect up to half of all literacy strugglers, as well as children who have no apparent literacy problems – so in simple economic terms this is an obvious strategy. (It will save thousands of pounds being spent on useless remediation.) The real gain to society, though, will be the countless children who progress easily through school, and go on to lead positive and fulfilled lives.

Conclusions

The jigsaw puzzle was, I felt, complete. All children had the ability to become fully literate, because all children had the intellectual ability to hear language and use it themselves. If a youngster experienced persistent literacy problems, the only possible reason had to be a perceptual disorder of some kind. Orton's left-right confusion gave rise to one particular kind of perceptual problem ('strephosymbolia'); and now Helen Irlen had identified another.

It couldn't be too difficult to tackle mere perceptual problems, could it? – and surely we owed our children nothing less.

V

Ways around the blockages

Dealing with dyslexia

Realizing that dyslexia is mainly a perceptual disorder, not a learning difficulty as such, or a lack of ability, makes it much easier to deal with. It is like a huge blockage in the children's path, and the trouble comes when teachers persist in trying to force their pupils through it. Not surprisingly, this leads to frustration for everyone. But there are ways around the blockage, and our task is to help dyslexic children travel by these routes.

Many youngsters struggle with reading and writing for the simple reason that they cannot refer to clear mental images of written words. So word recognition is difficult, spelling is a continual battle, and their handwriting is often badly formed and untidy because they cannot visualize how the words are supposed to look. What are the unblocked routes in these areas?

Understanding print

The good news is that there isn't only one form of word recognition, there are three – and two of them are just as straightforward for the 'word jumblers' as anybody.

If a child's primary school uses the 'look-and-say' approach to reading, when pupils are shown isolated written words, and expected to remember them before reading those same words in books, dyslexics will make little progress, because they cannot 'perform' to order.

We can certainly offer single words (preferably in bold red print at first, like Doman's early vocabularies) – but we concentrate on telling the children what they say all the time, or put labels on various objects in the room, so the meanings of the words are obvious. Doman points out that 'children love to learn but they do not love to be tested', and my credo is that we should 'test' children only when we are as certain as we can be that they are going to get the right answer. If written words are presented like this, it doesn't make any difference if they don't always match up with the child's mental images of them, because we are never putting the child on the spot, and expecting him to remember something when he doesn't.

As soon as a child has learned what written words are – patterns of shapes which convey meanings, and which can work together to produce sentences – an even better way of helping him to understand them is to read to him as much as possible, holding the book so he can follow the print. (Then, as I pointed out in the last chapter, a 'word jumbler' will gradually form mental clusters of words, like 'frog', 'forg' or 'grof' – all of which mean the same as the spoken word 'frog'. After a while the word 'frog' on the page matches with this cluster of words in the child's head, and he recognizes it straightaway.)

This is a brilliant method of helping all children to read. In 1976, Heinemann published *Young Fluent Readers*, by Margaret Clark, a study which set out to pinpoint the causes of success among thirty-two children who were already reading fluently and with understanding when they started school at five years old. How could it be that youngsters who had not attended school, and had never ploughed their way through all the stages of a graded reading scheme, were nevertheless reading silently and with total absorption, often at the 11-12 year old level, all manner of books including adult fiction?!

The common factor she discovered was that there was almost always at least one adult who had plenty of time to read to the child, listen to him and answer his questions. This adult rarely set out to teach the child to read, and was usually the one who did the reading at first – the child was seldom if ever required to read to the adult.

Extensive reading to my own daughters had underpinned all my work with them, and was, I felt sure, the main reason why they had learned to read independently with such speed.

It isn't difficult to establish the activity of reading aloud to children, while they follow the print, even in school. We can enlist parents' help to do this in a classroom, teachers can do it themselves, word-for-word tapes are a godsend, as I discovered – and parents can be encouraged to carry on with the whole thing at home. Here is the Reading Instruction Leaflet I offered to the parents of my literacy strugglers, at secondary level:

Reading Instruction Sheet

1. Help your child to choose a book he really wants to read. (A list of suggested books is available.) You can reject his choice if you wish (then you must choose another). But try to go along with it if you can.

2. You should both look for an attractive, enjoyable book, with super illustrations. The book should be a bit too difficult for him to manage on his own. (This is the exciting part.)

3. You read to him for about fifteen minutes. (You may need to read for longer if you are starting a new book, and want to get both of you into it.) *You* do this reading even if his own reading is quite good. You are sharing an enjoyable book together. Hold the book so he can see the print. Encourage him to follow as you read. If necessary run your pencil or finger under the words as you go.

4. Concentrate on enjoying what you are reading. Make it as dramatic as you can. Shout or growl for the angry bits. Whisper the frightening bits. Stop and talk about where the story is going, if you want. (Or discuss what the material is about, if it's more factual.)

5. When you reach a good stopping place, he reads back to you for about five minutes. He should read back the last couple of paragraphs you have read to him, if possible. If you think he would enjoy a more exciting bit from earlier on, you can re-read just that part to him. You want the meaning to be really fresh in his mind when he tackles it himself.

6. If he gets stuck on a word, give him a couple of seconds to think about it – then just tell him what the word says. Don't try to make him 'work it out'. (You will be helping him to 'work out' words later. It's very important not to bother him with all that at the beginning. Concentrate on enjoying the book.) He should repeat the word correctly, then carry on.

7. Praise him. Say things like, "That was super! That was fantastic! I never thought you were going to get that word right – and you did." Say things like, "Hey, that was incredible! I thought you were supposed to be bad at reading. You are not bad at all – you are *ace.*" Whenever he gets a word right that he got stuck on before, say, "Well done! You're learning it. That's excellent."

8. Praise him. (See above.)

9. Praise him. (See above.)

10. (It works!)

A certain amount of reading back is vital. Then we know the child is focusing on each word in turn, and having the experience of understanding it, as well as reading aloud correctly. It's much better than expecting a struggler to tackle some text 'cold', without reading it to him first. Don't worry that he will never be able to manage on his own: the time will come sooner than you think, when he takes charge of the book with a satisfied grin, and admonishes you, "Don't say anything, Mum, I can do it!"

Reading aloud

A word jumbler can learn to understand print fairly well by matching the words on the page with clusters of images of the same words in his head. He is seeing the meanings of the words directly, just like Wayne in the looking glass world I had imagined; and, again like Wayne, he may not be able to say them aloud. Or he could look at the word 'apple' and say 'fruit', getting pretty much the right meaning, but the wrong spoken word. This is all right as far as it goes – but it doesn't go nearly far enough.

The other kind of word recognition is to match a written word with the *spoken* recording of the word in the head. Saying written words aloud is extremely useful for hearing children beginning to read, as I pointed out in Chapter III, because it enables them to transfer meanings wholesale from their hearing vocabularies to print. Children who can match written words with spoken words, by themselves, very soon reach the point when they can understand in print anything they can understand in speech.

To a word jumbler, however, this form of word recognition is not just useful, it is a lifeline. Spoken words behave themselves for dyslexics to a much greater extent than written words do – evident from the fact that the youngsters can usually understand what they hear without any trouble, as well as talk intelligibly. They might muddle up a few spoken words, e.g. saying 'par cark' for 'car park', but on the whole speech is infinitely more reliable than print.

So matching print with speech means that a dyslexic child can bypass the visual jumble of the word in his head. For instance, suppose he is looking at the word 'frog'. He is 'seeing' it, mentally, as 'grof', (which doesn't yet form part of a useful cluster of visual images, all meaning the same thing). The word on the page won't match this mental version, and therefore he cannot recognize it that way. But if he has learned to sound out written words bit by bit, he can say "fŭ, frŭ, frŏ, frog" to himself – "oh, *frog!*" – and the words have matched perfectly.

This is why most reading programmes for dyslexics are unashamed phonic programmes – *Alpha to Omega,* by Bevé Hornsby and Frula Shear, or *Toe by Toe,* by Keda and Harry Cowling. The pupils learn phonics thoroughly and systematically, from the outset; and move on to reading books only when they have mastered the relevant phonics in every detail.

Unfortunately, the purpose of phonics has not been properly understood, either by the authors of these programmes, or by their critics on the 'whole language' side of the literacy debate. Both sides tend to assume that phonics is a matter of starting with the smallest possible bits (the letters of the alphabet), and learning how to put those bits together, slowly and painstakingly. The advocates of synthetic phonics maintain that this is what dyslexics particularly need to do, while the whole language camp say that this has precious little connection with reading for meaning, and relegate phonics to a very minor role indeed.

But phonics is best understood, not as putting the letters of the alphabet together, but as a *mapping procedure*. The child is learning to map a whole spoken word onto a whole written word, in such a way that the first sound in the spoken word maps onto the left hand edge of the written word, the last sound maps onto the right hand edge, and the middles map onto each other, bit by bit. (The child actually works from left to right along the written word, until he reaches the end, but the above description shows how the words are fitted to each other.) The procedure works with all words, even 'irregular' ones, e.g. 'thought':

The easiest way of helping a child to carry out this mapping procedure is by telling him the whole spoken word, first, then showing him how to match the pieces. E.g."This word says 'twig', doesn't it. We'll cover all the letters except the 't', look, and it just says 'tŭ'. Now it says 'tw'," [uncovering the 'w'] "now it says 'twĭ', now it says 'twig'. You do it."

Approaching phonics in terms of teaching a procedure, or technique, makes the whole thing plain sailing. There are only three steps:

1. First sound onto left hand edge.
2. Matching the ends and middles of words.
3. Blending the sounds.

In practice, you combine Steps 2 and 3, and help a child to blend the sounds as he goes along (see above).

Use an ordinary alphabet book to teach Step 1, with, say, a picture of an apple on one page, and the word 'apple' printed twice, opposite the picture, once beginning with a small letter, picked out in red, and once with a capital letter, also in red. It helps if the red letters are also printed by themselves, underneath the picture:

The child looks at the picture, and says 'apple'. He points to the two words, saying 'apple' both times, then to each initial letter, saying 'ă'. Finally he points to the separate letters underneath the picture, saying 'ă' again for each one.

It takes a few minutes at the most to learn this technique. After that it is practised with another twenty five words which, surprise surprise, just happen to begin with the other twenty five letters of the alphabet...

Steps 2 and 3 are readily taught as you show the children how to sound out a selection of three- and four-part words.

The children have now mastered the entire process of phonic matching. That is really all there is to it, but practice is key and needs to be carried out at every possible opportunity, until the technique has become instinctive.

In addition, youngsters need to know about the two main peculiarities of the English written system. One is that a single sound can match more than one letter (as in words like 'train', 'claw', 'graph', 'cloth', 'fight', etc.). Secondly, some letters are 'magic'. In certain conditions, the letters 'e', 'i' and 'y' particularly can change the sounds matching earlier letters.

You can also cover this territory very rapidly, and consolidate with practice, practice, practice. (See the Year Plan which follows Chapter VII.)

It is much simpler to get to grips with the sounding out procedure if you stop thinking about the separate letters in words, and concentrate instead on the separate sounds. You are building up a spoken word sound by sound, and matching each successive sound with the equivalent letter or letters in the written word. (This is why the procedure works with all words, whether they are 'irregular' or not.) Practise with any number of spoken words by themselves (i.e. without matching them with written words at first), and it will all start making beautiful sense. E.g.'kŭ, kĭ, kitch, kitchĕ, kitchen', 'shŭ, shĕ, shel, shelv, shelves', 'wŭ, wor, walk', 'shŭ, shă, sham, shamp, shampoo', 'cŭ, că, cărr, carrĭ, carriage'.

Because you always begin by telling your pupil what the whole written word says, *then* help him to sound it out, he will never be confused, but just go on copying you until he can manage independently. In a matter of months, he will be able to match written words with spoken words, and transfer meanings from one form of language to the other, whenever he wishes.

(If you are working with your own child at home, you might like to know that I have produced packs of phonic word cards and an accompanying booklet, *As Easy as ABC: Phonic Analysis in Two Terms*, enabling you to teach the complete phonic programme. Details at the end of this book.)

Spelling

The interesting thing is that when you read to a child, holding the book so he can see the print, you are using spoken words to help provide the meanings for the written words, very rapidly. When he reads back some of the text, he is doing the same thing, matching whole written words with whole spoken words.

At first, you just correct him if he makes a mistake. But as he goes on learning phonics, you can ask him to sound out the words he is doubtful about, with plenty of help from you to make sure he gets them right. "Oh, that's a word with a short vowel," [I call them 'vowel sandwiches', an instantly memorable term] "cover it up and sound it out – hŭ, hă, han, hand – well done!" "This word has a two-letter sound at the end, look – 'ph' saying 'fŭ'. Tŭ, tĕ, tĕl, tĕlĕ, telegŭ, telegrŭ, telegră, telegraph. Excellent!" Or "There's a magic 'i' in this one, making the 'c' say 'sŭ' – ă, ac, acs, acsĭ, accidŭ, accidĕ, acciden, accident. Clever old you."

Then you can ask him to tackle small amounts of unfamiliar text, again offering help, but encouraging him to work out the words by himself. He will steadily continue to take over, until you might even be able to persuade him to read you the occasional bedtime story, if you're tired…

The more reading aloud he does, the better; he should do some every day if he can. It is the practice he needs – each time he reads aloud, the written words are glueing themselves more and more firmly to their matching spoken words, until he can see their meanings, *and* what they say, as soon as he looks at them.

Reading aloud is a useful skill in its own right, but it is also the best possible basis for accurate spelling. This is because the process of writing is the mirror image of the process of reading aloud!

When we read aloud, we look at the words on the page, and match them with the words we say. When we write, on the other hand, we usually say the words to ourselves, under our breath, and match those spoken words with the ones we are writing.

So if we are accustomed to matching written words with spoken words, bit by bit, while we read, it is very easy to reverse the process, and also match the two forms of language, bit by bit, while we write. The letters in a word automatically arrange themselves in the proper order, because it is the same order as the sounds in the spoken word.

This is clearly a tremendous help for the word jumblers. A youngster can say 'fŭ', and write an 'f'; 'frŭ', and write an 'r'; 'frŏ', and write an 'o'; 'frog', and write the 'g'. It doesn't matter if the visual form of the word is muddling itself up inside his head: he can use the sounds in the spoken word to straighten it out again, and make it behave.

A child who has worked through my phonic programme, and practised reading aloud until he is fluent, can therefore spell all regular words correctly without any trouble. We just need to make sure that he does sound out words, whenever he writes, and matches the letters to the sounds. (Which explains why it is a good idea for him to spend time occasionally sounding out spoken words by themselves, as described above: the experience will pay off in spades when it comes to writing, and he needs to begin by thinking of the sounds first, then match them with letters.)

Many dyslexic children find this solution to the spelling problem after years of desperate struggle to spell words 'the way they look', and realizing that it doesn't work. Spelling words 'the way they sound', instead, means that at least you have letters for all the sounds in a word, following the same order, so you can re-read what you have written; even if your spelling doesn't quite agree with the dictionary version.

There remains the question of what to do about irregular words. I was trying to help eleven-year-old Troy discover an answer. "If words that are spelt the way they sound are called 'regular' words, Troy," I fished, "what shall we call the others, the ones that aren't?" I was hoping he might decide on 'irregular', but Troy looked at me with venom written all over his small face, and responded bitterly, "I'm going to call them *sneaks*." So 'sneaks' they became, for ever after.

It's surprisingly easy to deal with the sneaks – most of us have always known how, without consciously realizing it. When we tackle a real maverick of a word, like 'Wednesday', we alter the way we say it, first. We say 'Wed-nes-day' to ourselves, inside our heads, and each bit of the word comes out right.

What we have done is to change 'Wednesday' into a regular word! It doesn't occur to us to say 'Wed-nes-day' when we're talking to someone. But the alternative pronunciation is available for use when we're writing.

If we can do it with three or four words – 'temper-a-ture', 'par-li-a-ment', 'Feb-ru-ary' – we can do it with hundreds. The human mind can store an infinitely large spoken vocabulary, and an infinitely large reading vocabulary. It can just as well store a third vocabulary, parallel to the first two. A 'saying-for-spelling vocabulary', which all children compile if they find it helpful, so that anybody with problems will thereby have the means of choosing the right spelling. 'Bee-cay-use' (because), 'pe-op-lee' (people), 'ee-nor-mō-us' (enormous), 'ex-tinc-tī-on', 'dee-kī-sī-on', 'wăl-king', 'brid-ge', 'sō-und', 'trot-ting, (so the double letter won't go missing) – well, you get the idea. It's surprising how easily children can work out and remember these repronunciations, once they've had enough initial practice; and also mnemonics for the really awkward letter patterns: 'old uncles go hang-gliding' (ough), 'old uncles like doughnuts' (ould), 'indians get hot' (igh), or 'all unicorns grow horns' (augh).

The basic theme is storing a way of saying any word which will give you the spelling – and then making sure that you think of the sounds while you're writing. It's an effective and reliable means of bypassing the spelling problem. So how can we make it readily available to all children who need it?

The easiest way of bringing this about is to make sure that the spelling dragon never has even the slightest chance of getting a grip – by teaching all children to operate the Key to Sound Spelling right from the start of their writing experience. (See next page.)

Dyslexics who can use this Key, whenever they write, have every chance of growing up to spell just as accurately as their peers. It's also a very handy aid to spelling for *any* child, so nothing is lost by teaching it to whole classes of young children.

These 'saying-for-spelling' versions of words form a series of spelling cues, ensuring that youngsters can not only spell words correctly, they will *know* they are spelling correctly. As long as the words they write reflect the spelling cues in their heads, they know the spellings are accurate. I often say to my students, "Isn't it lovely, you don't have to learn any more spellings, all you have to learn are the spelling cues, which are much easier." Children can be quite demoralized when I start working with them, resigned to scoring 2 out of 10 on their school spelling tests. "Would you like to get 10 out of 10, every time?" I ask, and they look at me as if to say, "Pigs might fly." But we work through the list of spellings for their next test, thinking of cues, and when I see them again I ask casually, "Well, what did you get?" They try not to grin, to be nonchalant, but the corners of their mouths twitch. "Oh, 10 out of 10," they say airily – knowing, now, they can score full marks on their spelling tests whenever they want.

THE KEY TO 'SOUND' SPELLING

LOOK at the word and ask:

① Does it tally? (Is it spelt the way it sounds?)
If YES – tally it while you write it.

If NO – go to Step 2.

* ② Can you make it tally? (Chunk it and 're-say' each chunk. E.g. Wed-nes-day.)
If YES – make it tally; tally it while you write it.

If NO – go to Step 3.

③ Think of a mnemonic.
E.g. ough – old uncles get heavy
ould – old uncles like driving
igh – indians get hot
augh – all unicorns grow horns
Say the mnemonic to yourself while you write the word. E.g. 'n – indians get hot – t'

---

* For Step 2 – Identify the 'sneaky bits' in the word before you think of cues. The THREE SNEAKS are:

SNEAK 1 – Silent letters – must be said (e.g. lat-e, lam-b)

SNEAK 2 – Double letters – say sound twice (e.g. trot-ting)

SNEAK 3 – Letters making a different sound – say ordinary sound
(e.g. wō-měn)

You can see why practice in reading aloud is such a necessary foundation for correct spelling. In fact as your child's reading becomes more assured, it is an excellent plan to allow him to attempt the really difficult words, even if he mispronounces them at first. 'Te(t)ch-no-log-y' he might say, and you correct him – but there are the spelling cues for the word, already in place for later use.

Intervening with older children

On the spelling front, as on all others, prevention before intervention is the ideal, but if the problem has become entrenched, you have to intervene as rapidly and as positively as you can. Dyslexics become more and more frustrated by their (largely futile) struggles with spelling the older they get, and this could colour their whole attitude to school and school work. Each subject seems to demand increasing amounts of writing; and for someone who cannot spell, whose every piece of work is substandard in that respect, school may well constitute a never ending assault on their self esteem. (Not surprising, is it, if it's the poor spellers who bunk off school in grimly disaffected swathes – and we all know what *that* can lead to.)

You want to show them how to tackle their own spelling errors, rather than learning lists of words which someone else has chosen; but one thing they are good at, by now, is avoiding writing difficult words. So their free writing doesn't furnish as many spelling mistakes as you would like!

I dealt with that one by screening all the incoming Year 7s, using the following diagnostic dictation, taken from Margaret Peters' *Diagnostic and Remedial Spelling Manual*. It contains exactly 100 words (so working out percentages when scoring is easy), and covers a wide variety of spelling patterns. Poor spelling is immediately obvious. Another useful feature is that children with reading difficulties almost always have spelling problems as well – you have therefore identified most of the literacy strugglers with this one test. (The remainder should be revealed when you screen for Irlen Syndrome – see Chapter VI.) Reassure the children, before they write out the passage, that spelling problems often go hand-in-hand with high intelligence and unusual gifts, and not to worry if they make several spelling mistakes:

> Late one night my friend woke me, saying, "Would you enjoy a trial-run in my new helicopter?"
> I had scarcely scrambled into my track-suit before we were away. The lights of the city glowed beneath, the stars above. I was beginning to wonder about our destination when I caught sight of the spinning knife edge and the surface of what must have been a type of flying saucer whistling round us. We dodged skilfully to avoid an accident. To our relief, the space-craft regained height, and we sank down to earth and the comfortable bed I had never actually left.

Now you can teach a spelling struggler to use the Key to Sound Spelling, by thinking of and learning cues for words that he himself spelled incorrectly. This means individual tuition, but it is quite straightforward to arrange for pupils to work in pairs, and tutor each other; or train parents as tutors, in your after-school literacy club.

The idea is that the learner writes out each misspelled word, correctly, three times, saying the cues while he writes. Most older children, though, find it much more exciting and grown-up to type the words instead of writing them – see section on **Typing skills**, below.

Enlarge the passage to A4, and copy onto coloured paper (pale yellow is a good choice), for the benefit of children with Irlen Syndrome. If you can use blue print or something similar, so much the better. The student refers to this original copy to find the correct spellings he needs.

The procedure for the tutor goes something like this: Help your pupil to find his first spelling mistake, in his 'working document', and compare it with the version in the original. His initial task is to identify the letters he got *right* – you want to boost his self-confidence from the outset. Then suggest a reason for his own spelling. E.g. Suppose he has written 'lat' for 'late'. You could say, "Well, the letters you've written are correct, *and* they are letters for all the sounds in the word. The only thing that needs adding is the silent 'e' at the end – you left that out because you couldn't see it in your head, and you can't hear it because it's silent. But if you say 'lăt-ē, you'll always remember to put the 'e' in, won't you. 'Go Home'," [i.e. place your fingers on the home keys of the typewriter/word processor] "say 'lat' and type 'lat'. Look at the keyboard all you want to, just make sure you use the right fingers. Now say 'ē' and type the 'e'. Type a comma (to practise using commas), and type the word again. Repeat the cues after me just before you type each bit. Now type the word a third time, saying each cue yourself. Look back at the words already typed if you forget the cues." (You are trying to make it quite impossible for him to get the word wrong.)

Another example: If he has written 'nite' for 'night', say, "Well, your spelling is so much more sensible than the original, isn't it. That's just the way a lot of people think the word *should* be spelled. Who would have expected 'igh' in the middle?! How about saying 'indians get hot' for that bit? Then the cues for 'night' will be 'n-indians get hot-t' – and you can use 'indians get hot' for any word with 'igh' in it." He types the word three times, saying the cues as before.

Before going further, he should look at the word he has just typed, saying the cues (with gaps between the bits); then the word above it, and the one above that, until he has repeated cues for all the words he has typed in that session. Remind him to *look* at each word while he says the cues. Most children think they should be repeating the cues from memory, and look away; so explain that you want him to link the way the word looks on the screen with the cues he is saying.

The learner repeats the cues in this way every time he adds a new word. Then he has an excellent chance of remembering most of them, with a little further practice.

Spelling notebook

Don't type the cues themselves, but after the session write each word learned in a spelling notebook, followed by the cues. Review these cues at the beginning of the next session, again beginning at the bottom of the list. The learner looks at the words on the left hand side of the page, while he says the cues, but can glance over at the cues any time he needs to. *Then* ask him to repeat the cues from memory.

Typing each sentence

As soon as your pupil has learned all the words for a complete sentence, review them as described, and dictate the sentence for him to type. Tell him the punctuation, and show him how to include speech marks, etc. Just before he types each word learned, he repeats the cues (looking at the word on the screen if he needs to). You are not testing his memory, but giving him the experience of spelling the words correctly, and thinking of the cues while typing. The more he does this when working with you, the more likely he is to remember the relevant cues when he is writing independently. Work on the first sentence could look something like this:

late, late, late,
night, night, night,
friend, friend, friend,
woke, woke, woke,
would, would, would,
helicopter, helicopter, helicopter,

Late one night my friend woke me, saying, "Would you enjoy a trial-run in my new helicopter?"

Carry on in this way (keeping the sessions fairly short), until the youngster has mastered all the words he got wrong. Then he types the entire passage from dictation, in the same way that he typed each sentence.

He might like to frame the printout, as he has every reason to feel very proud of himself.

Encourage him to use the words learned, in his own writing. The more he practises, the more confident his spelling will become.

Review the Key to Sound Spelling

Now is the best time to review the Key to Sound Spelling. Your pupil has already discovered how to use it while tackling the dictation passage, so it will be very easy for him to understand the three steps, and memorize the sneaks for Step 2. Point out that one of the three steps will work for any possible word, and he should operate the Key from now on, whenever he is learning a tricky word.

(Remind him to use Step 2 – repronunciation – as much as he can. Simplest is best. Keep mnemonics in reserve for the real spelling horrors.)

Suggested spelling cues for 'Late one night' dictation

Here is a list of spelling cues for the 'Late one night' dictation. These are suggestions only – a pupil might well think of alterations to make them easier for him to remember.

late –	lăt/ē (to underline the 'e's function. Steer the children away from 'lā/tē' for this reason, but 'sŏ/mē' would be appropriate for 'some'.)
night –	n/<u>i</u>ndians get <u>h</u>ot/t
friend –	frī/end (Who's your best friend? Well, don't tell him, but you're going to *fri [fry]* him, sizzle, sizzle, and sadly that will be the *end* of him.)

woke –	wŏk/ē
would –	w/<u>o</u>ld <u>u</u>ncles <u>l</u>ike <u>d</u>oughnuts
new –	<u>n</u>ever <u>e</u>at <u>w</u>eeds
helicopter –	hē/lī/cop/ter
scarcely –	s/car/c/ely, or a mnemonic like '<u>s</u>mall <u>c</u>ars <u>a</u>nd <u>r</u>acing <u>c</u>ars <u>e</u>at <u>l</u>arge <u>y</u>oghurts'
scrambled –	sc/ram/blĕd
track –	sound it out: tŭ, trŭ, tră, trăc, track
suit –	sū/ĭt
before –	B for E (boyfriend and girlfriend)
were –	wer/ē, or just 'no h'
beneath –	Benjamin Edward Ath – Ben E. Ath for short – standing *beneath* a tree
stars –	s/tar/s
above –	ā/bŏv/ē
beginning –	beg/in/ning, or begin/ning. (Don't chunk a word any more than you have to.)
our –	Oh you are (O/U/R) *clever* (in a whisper)
destination –	des/tin/ā/tī/on. (If you don't have a 'tie on', your *destination* is probably the Head's office.)
caught –	c/<u>a</u>ll <u>u</u>nicorns grow <u>h</u>orns/t
sight –	like 'night'
spinning –	spin/ning, like beginning
knife –	k/nĭf/ē
surface –	"You are" (to remind about the 'u') "Sur Face!" or surf/ace
type –	Why type? (to remind about the 'y')
saucer –	sā/ū/ker, or sound it out: sŭ, sau, sauk, sauce, saucer
skilfully –	skil/ful/ly. Join skill and full, drop an 'l' from each. Add 'ly'.
avoid –	a/vŏ/id
accident –	ac/kid/ent, or ac/kī/dent
relief –	rē/lī/ēf
space –	spac/ē

height –	hē/indians get hot/t, or h/eight (if the child knows 'eight')
earth –	ear/th
comfortable –	cŏm/for/table
actually –	ac/tu/al/ly

And so on. Incidentally, since the procedure is to say a doubled letter twice (spin-ning), you know when you have only one letter, because you say it only once.

Teenagers and adults

You can follow the very same approach with teenagers and adults, but use a dictation passage better suited to their interest level. Here is a more advanced one, again from Margaret Peters' *Diagnostic and Remedial Spelling Manual:*

> A peculiar shape was approaching from the southern valley. Gradually they distinguished a recently designed aeroplane circling above.
>
> The machine touched down with precision in the rough mountainous region, without even scraping its surface. The children surrounded the pilot, who explained that his altimeter and temperature gauge were damaged, and he was anxious about increasing altitude in these freezing conditions. From the alpine school he telephoned his base, requesting spare instruments to be delivered and fitted immediately.
>
> The children viewed the repairs with enthusiasm, especially when they were taken in groups for an unforgettable flight before the pilot's final departure.

Work out spelling cues as for the 'Late one night' dictation. The main thing is to deal with the 'three sneaks': say silent letters (shap-ē); say double letters twice (ap-pro-ach-ing); and for letters making a different sound, say the ordinary sound (e-spek-ī-al-ly). If the student says "Why won't I spell it with a 'k' if I say it like that?" point out that of course he won't, because he knows that 'k' can never go with an 's' sound. He is trying to choose between an 's' and a 'c' – 'k' isn't even in the running.

Chunk words in line with their meanings whenever possible: i.e. split 'especially' before the second 'l', rather than saying 'e-spek-i-all-y'. That gives you cues for 'special' as well as 'especially'; plus it helps you to explain how to make adjectives into adverbs, by adding 'ly'. Also, offer cues like 'mō-unt' for the first part of 'mountainous' only if the student has had difficulty with that part of the word, otherwise offer 'mount-ā-in-o-us', or 'moun-tā-in-o-us' (to separate the consonants 'n' and 't' – adjacent consonants can be a problem). Cues should always be based on the pupil's own particular mistakes.

If chunking really doesn't work, go for a mnemonic. E.g. 'circle' is a bit awkward, so suggest 'cheese is rotten, can't like everything' while picturing a round and mouldy cheese. Cues for 'circling' could then be 'circ-ling', or 'cheese is rotten, can't like it, no good'.

Work on dictation – summary of procedure

1.   Look at working document.

2.   Find first spelling error.

3.   Look at original document, find correct spelling.

4.   Identify sneaks – THINK OF CUES for word.

5.   Type word three times, with commas, say cues while typing. Press ENTER.

6.   Repeat for next spelling error.

7.   REVIEW CUES FOR BOTH WORDS. LOOK AT WORDS.

8.   Repeat for all errors in first sentence. Review all cues as each word is added.

9.   Review all cues. Type sentence from dictation. Review cues for each word before typing.

The ACE Spelling Dictionary

When learning new spellings, the first essential is the word itself, correctly spelled, so your pupil needs rapid access to these correct spellings.

This can pose something of a problem. A child might ask an adult for a spelling, and the adult might reply, "Look it up in a dictionary." To which any spelling struggler's response could well be, "How can I look it up in a dictionary if I don't know how to spell it?"

He has a point! Look for the word 'pneumonia' in a conventional dictionary, and you will probably never find it, because you are looking under 'N'.

The *ACE* (Aurally Coded English) *Spelling Dictionary,* published by LDA, is very differently organized, and you really can track down almost any word, by sounding it out. It takes a little while to get the hang of using the Dictionary (especially for adults...), but the strugglers find it such a boost to their morale that it is well worth the time and effort involved. I now maintain that you always go to the ACE Dictionary when you are looking for a spelling; you use an ordinary dictionary when you already know the spelling, and want to check on the meaning. Piece of cake!

As soon as you have found a word in the ACE Dictionary, think of spelling cues, and write it in the back of your spelling notebook, so you never have to look it up again. E.g. the cues for 'pneumonia' could be 'p-nē-u-monia' (saying the silent letters).

Electronic spellmasters (about the size of a calculator) work in the same way as the Dictionary, and older pupils often prefer them. However, show them how to use the ACE Dictionary as well – it is more reliable and has more information.

Handwriting

Cursive handwriting is a form of joined writing particularly recommended for dyslexics, because it can be learned 'by the feel', and therefore does not have to be visualized accurately. Each word is written as a whole, without lifting the pen/pencil, so the fingers steadily remember the spellings!

Here is a cursive handwriting sheet (see next page):

Every letter (lower case) begins on the bottom line, which again makes it easier to learn. This means an initial stroke for each letter, as shown – 'rainbows' for letters that start with a curve, 'rockers' for the ones that don't. (These initial strokes can be abandoned later, as the pupil develops his own personal style, but they are helpful at the start.)

Capital letters begin at the top, and are drawn – i.e. you can lift your pencil between strokes. So the feeling of writing them is quite different. Also, you don't join on to capital letters – this helps dyslexics to avoid the common mistake of writing capital letters in the middles of words: the feeling of writing them like that is wrong.

Cursive writing is best practised on good old-fashioned handwriting paper, printed in 'tram lines'. (You can write to me, at One-to-One Publications, for a pack of photocopiable record sheets, including masters for handwriting paper.) Then the children learn how to line up the tops and bottoms of their letters, how to produce writing of a uniform size, and to appreciate the difference between tall letters, short letters, and long ones.

Joined writing is actually easier to learn than printing, so it is a good plan to teach it first, to all children (see my Year Plan, in the Appendix).

HANDWRITING SHEET

c rainbow   v u-shaped connector
J rocker   ⌣ saucer connector

a b c d e f g h i
j k l m n o p q r
s t u v w x y z

abcdefghijklmnopqrstuvwxyz

The quick brown fox jumps over
the lazy dog.

A B C D E F G H I
J K L M N O P Q R
S T U V W X Y Z

Typing skills

Learning to type, using the proper fingers, is greatly beneficial for dyslexics. As with cursive handwriting, it is learned by the feel, and therefore the fingers remember the spellings. It is a useful and marketable skill in its own right, so has much more kudos than spelling lessons as such. I always began work on spelling by teaching my students to type – quite often I was waylaid by indignant Year 7s who wanted to be included in my typing programme: "My spelling is awful, Miss, honestly it is!"

Typing is automatically a multi-sensory approach to spelling. The pupil says the cues while he types (saying and hearing), he sees the correct word on the screen, and he has the feeling of typing the right letters in the right order.

You *can* teach Sound Spelling without typing, and there will always be the occasional child who doesn't want to learn to type. But since for most youngsters it is a lot of fun, here is a way of training a roomful of typists, without having to resort to lengthy and meaningless drills (and even if you don't type yourself...). Use computer keyboards, manual typewriters, or keyboard diagrams (A4 size). The pupils can look at the keyboard all they want to, they must just make sure they always use the right fingers. (Later, they can move on to touch typing proper – typing without looking at the keyboard.) The approach described here ensures that they learn to operate the complete keyboard very rapidly.

Agree on the same names for the fingers – little finger, ring finger, middle finger, index (or pointing) finger.

"Look at the keyboard – how many rows of letters (not numbers) are there? Three – good. The middle row of letters is called the 'home keys', because it is where your fingers live. Place all your fingers on the home keys now, one finger on each key. The G and the H must be left empty – reminding your fingers to Go Home. Your index fingers live on the F and the J, and on a computer you will feel a little raised dot on those keys, letting you know your fingers are in the right places. Your thumbs do not live on any letters, their job is to operate the space bar.

"Beginning with the little finger of your left hand, type the letters a, s, d and f. Now your index (pointing) finger reaches across to type the g (you can move your whole hand), and returns to live on the F. Type the f again. Operate the space bar with your left thumb.

"The little finger of your right hand types the ; then type l, k and j. Your index finger reaches across to type the h (again, you should move your whole hand), and returns to the J key. Type j again. Operate the space bar with your right thumb, and press RETURN/ENTER. (Or come down to the next line, if using a manual typewriter.)

"Take your hands off the keyboard, and look at the whole keyboard again. In addition to the three rows of letters going across, you can also see them as ten columns slanting down from left to right, with three keys in each column. One of your fingers is responsible for typing the letters in each of the columns.

"Look at the QAZ column. Which finger do you think is responsible for that one? Yes, that's right, the little finger of your left hand. Put your hands on the home keys. Now your whole hand moves up, type the q with your little finger, move your whole hand down and type the a, move your whole hand down and type the z. Move back to the a, and type it again. Operate the space bar with your left thumb."

(Repeat for all the other columns, asking your pupils to begin a new line when they start the columns for the right hand.)

When operating a machine, their typing practice will look like this:

asdfgf ;lkjhj
qaza wsxs edcd rfvf tgbg
p;/; ol.l ik,k ujmj yhnh

Even young children can learn these skills after only a few sessions. Then they can look at the keyboard straightaway, while they type, but they must work out which finger is going to do the job, *before* typing any letter. Their task is to train their fingers properly, bearing in mind their fingers will try to get away with murder, given half a chance! If the wrong finger types a letter, they must be firm, delete it, and type it again with the proper finger.

After that, frequent practice (copying some of their favourite poems or stories, and using the Key to Sound Spelling to help them learn any difficult spellings) will soon ensure that every youngster is typing rapidly and correctly.

Extended writing

Learning to type has all sorts of advantages, quite apart from helping with spelling. Making corrections and alterations is much easier on a word processor than on a page of writing (or using a manual typewriter). So dyslexics can produce a finished piece of work which looks good and does them justice, without having to expend the blood, sweat and tears that often go into ordinary writing. Even if a first draft is handwritten, a student knows he can type the final version, and take pride in it.

'Copy typing' – typing out a passage from a favourite book – practises skills already learned, and teaches new ones. The youngster is reading the text, hopefully understanding it, and also reading it aloud under his breath in order to copy it. The agreement is that he copies word by word, never letter by letter: he looks at each word, decides on spelling cues if necessary, looks away from the text and types it from memory. (If he can copy three or four words at once, that is even better.) He must re-

read each sentence on the screen as soon as it's completed, and check to make sure it is correct.

Then, copy typing is the most painless way I know of learning punctuation skills. The typist is inevitably having the experience of using full stops, commas, question marks, apostrophes and speech marks in the right places, as well as setting out the text in paragraphs. This provides an excellent foundation for learning how to punctuate his own work.

It is so easy that it almost seems like cheating, but don't overlook the activity on that account: learning to read and write should be as easy as possible. What is happening is that the youngster is serving an apprenticeship to a master craftsman – he is thinking the author's thoughts alongside him, and watching the same words come out of his fingers, with all the right punctuation signs doing their proper jobs. An apprenticeship is the best way of learning any craft, so let's make full use of the approach when it comes to writing.

A child who has learned to type, how to think of and remember spelling cues, and how to use the *ACE Spelling Dictionary*, has all the basic skills he needs for producing acceptable work. The next step is to help him use these skills when writing himself.

As soon as he has finished learning the spellings for one of the dictation passages, and can find his way around in the ACE Dictionary, I wheedle a written piece out of him. Quite a good way of achieving this, if his parent is involved, is for him to dictate a story or essay to Mum or Dad. The parent dictates it back to the child on another occasion. This means that the youngster focuses on only one process at a time: composing the piece in the first instance, followed later on by the physical process of getting it down on paper. But it's still all his own work, and his own writing.

After that, he and I need to make any necessary corrections. We tackle the spelling first. I will underline all the spelling errors, he finds the words in the ACE Dictionary, thinks of spelling cues, and records them in his spelling notebook.

Punctuation comes next. Often schools expect children to be able to punctuate their work, without really explaining what the punctuation signs mean, and how to use them. In Appendix 4 (p.169), you will find a Proofreading Guide that I have written, which my students find very helpful. Please feel free to photocopy it if you would like to.

When a youngster is learning how to use the Guide, don't expect him to correct every mistake in his writing at once. That is too daunting. Work through the Guide one point at a time – put in full stops and capital letters first, then question marks and exclamation marks (if any), then commas, and so on. Review the punctuation rules previously learned at the beginning of each session, and in this way your pupil will steadily make the Guide his own.

It is a good idea to practise using the Guide by correcting a passage containing all the points listed. You might like to have a look at *The Craft of Writing,* my manual for Key Stage 3 teachers, (Year 7+), with lots of photocopiable worksheets on spelling, punctuation, grammar, proofreading, dictionary skills, typing and handwriting. One of the worksheets is a passage with no punctuation at all. Help your student to work through it step by step, following the Guide, and produce a perfectly typed version when he has finished. (See list of books and materials at the end of this book.)

Telling the time

An analogue clock is one where the hands go round the face, in the same way that the sun (apparently) goes round the earth. Dyslexics often have trouble telling the time on an analogue clock, because their mental images of the clock face get jumbled up, (like written words), making it difficult for them to 'recognize' the time.

Reading the time on a digital clock is easier, so long as they focus on the digits from left to right, and say them aloud at first (just as phonics and reading aloud help with word recognition).

Through practice, however, dyslexics can learn to tell the time on analogue clocks as well. Initially they have to work out what the hands are telling them, instead of recognizing their positions, but this process can become quite speedy.

I usually start right at the beginning, with a globe and a torch (to represent the sun). As the globe spins, a complete day (one revolution) is divided into day time and night time. An appreciation of day and night was our first time division as human beings. Ever since then, we have been learning how to split time up into steadily decreasing 'lengths', depending on what we need to compare those lengths with.

After day and night, our next step was the division into morning and afternoon. In the morning, the sun was climbing upwards, while after noon it was going downwards, towards evening.

For thousands of years this division was sufficient for us to carry on our daily lives. But as those lives became more complicated, we wanted smaller chunks of time for measuring our activities. We split the morning and the afternoon into hours, and invented sundials to mark their passage.

The hour hand on a clock is like the shadow on a sundial: it takes twelve hours to go right round the clock face. (Spend some time demonstrating this, and counting the hours from 12 to 12. It helps if your pupil can physically move the hour hand himself.)

Then we realized that an hour was too long if, say, we wanted to arrange a meeting. Telling someone that you will meet him 'in the third hour' means that one of you could well be hanging around for fifty-nine minutes. So the hours themselves had to be split up into shorter units. We decided to divide an hour into sixty minutes (ask your pupil to count the minutes, preferably in fives), and included a minute hand to measure these new units. How long does it take the minute hand to go right round the clock? That's right, sixty minutes, or one hour. When the minute hand is coming down past the 12, the time is a certain number of minutes *past* the hour. When the minute hand is travelling up towards the 12, the time is a certain number of minutes *to* the next hour. (This motion is called 'clockwise'; going the other way is 'anti-clockwise'.)

After that, it's fairly plain sailing. The youngster looks at the hour hand first, and decides which is the nearest hour. Then he decides whether the minute hand is coming down past the 12, or going up to it. Finally he decides on the number of minutes past or to the hour. (To help children learn, some clocks have these minutes written in small figures, i.e. 5 beside the 1, 10 beside the 2, etc. If yours doesn't, take off the cover and write them in! Write 15 *and* quarter past beside the 3; half past beside the 6; 15 and quarter to beside the 9.)

Prompt the child by reminding him of these steps, but as soon as possible encourage him to remember them himself. Ask him to look at a clock and tell you the time, saying 'No' encouragingly if he makes a mistake, and waiting for him to put it right. Help him out if he gets in a real muddle, but carry on telling him that you know he can do it by himself. He soon will.

Learning the alphabet, days of the week, months of the year, timelines
More mental maps that wriggle themselves around when your child isn't looking! At the secondary school where I worked, I used to be responsible for the lower school library. One lad whose spelling was wild and wonderful borrowed a book towards the end of September. "When do I return it, Miss?" I checked to

see. "The tenth of October, Darrell." But he was still puzzled. "When *is* October, Miss?"

That was my first indication that there was more to this dyslexia business than difficulties with reading and writing. The root cause, though, is the same. The child cannot 'see' the order of the letters, days and months in his head. So what are the ways around the blockages for these things?

We could do a lot worse than go back to good old fashioned chanting. It is received wisdom these days to dismiss recitation as mere 'rote learning' – but there is a great deal to be said for rote learning. It means that a child can refer to a *spoken* map of the alphabet, days of the week and months of the year, to help make up for the deficiencies in the visual one.

During their early primary school years, children are brilliant at learning by heart. Alphabets, tables, poems, you name it, they can learn it. I absorbed most of the New Testament as a child, quite naturally (because my father is a minister), and now I am in my sixties, it is still there to cheer me on my way. (*Though I speak with the tongues of men and of angels, and have not charity, I am become as sounding brass or a tinkling cymbal...*) I barely understood most of it when I was little – understanding kept unfolding itself later on, as the years passed, but the words were safely in place by then, thank heaven. The same with tables – *after* I had learned them it dawned on me that multiplication was repeated addition. Aha, so that's why eight sevens are fifty-six!

Those so-called 'old fashioned' teachers knew exactly what they were doing. They were capitalizing on children's ability to learn by heart to provide them with resources which would illuminate their minds and nourish their souls for the rest of their lives.

Sadly, this ability fades with time, and in great measure is left behind with childhood. Try to teach secondary level strugglers to recite the alphabet, or tables, and you might as well not bother:

they can't do it. Learning by heart is satisfying, easy and fun for little children – so please, please, please let's reintroduce it into every primary school, a.s.a.p.

Such spoken maps are not enough by themselves, but they go a long way towards providing a solid, reliable foundation. In addition, we need to think of any other possible means for making these sequences accessible to all children.

It is well known that dyslexics benefit from a multi-sensory approach to learning. (It is not the 'multi'ness that makes the difference, however, so much as offering children alternative routes, which do not depend on being able to visualize clear mental images.)

In *The Gift of Dyslexia,* Ron Davis suggests a helpful way for a child to master the alphabet, by making the letters in clay, both upper and lower case. The youngster recites the alphabet, slowly, forwards and backwards, touching each letter as he goes along. He does further exercises with his clay alphabet(s), until he is certain of the order. If your child is having any problems learning the alphabet, it is well worth consulting Davis' book in this respect – as in many others.

The authors of *Alpha to Omega,* 'the A-Z of teaching reading, writing and spelling' to dyslexics, have garnered several amusing rhymes dealing with days of the week and months of the year. One is the deliciously gloomy recitation of the months by Michael Flanders, ending 'Dark November brings the fog, Should not do it to a dog. Breezy wet December then – Bloody January again!' Do encourage your child to learn these verses by heart – I guarantee he will enjoy them.

Another book of poems crying out to be declaimed aloud, even acted in costume, is *Kings and Queens,* by Eleanor and Herbert Farjeon. John Julius Norwich wrote of it: 'I was quite literally brought up on these brilliant verses. My mother gave me a shilling for every one I learnt by heart and I can still recite most of them. They contain everything a child needs to know about our kings and queens, bringing each one unforgettably to life. Parents will ignore them at their peril.' (I am similarly bribing my grandchildren to learn them – with inflation the price has increased to 50p per poem.) All the poems are historically accurate, but very funny. You learn the date for each monarch, so end up with a most useful mental timeline for English history. Any further historical books can be assigned to their proper place in the sequence of events: 'Oh, that's when Richard I was King.' A book to be savoured and remembered with pleasure.

Multiplication tables

It does children no harm at all to recite their tables, and the sooner the better. Then those useful aids will be available for multiplication and division as the youngsters progress through the school system. (They should recite the whole thing – i.e. '1 two is 2, 2 twos are 4' etc., not just count in twos. As a result, with any luck, they will hear themselves saying '7 twos are 14' when that information is needed quickly.)

The snag is that sooner or later mere recitation lets you down. If you cannot picture the 7s table, say, unfolding in your mind when another 7 is added on, and if there are sudden holes in the spoken map to boot, you are up the creek without a paddle. Your only recourse is to recite the table again, from the beginning, hoping that this time it will come out right. Of course if you do make a mistake, but overlook it, the rest of your table will probably be wrong as well.

There is another way. You can look at multiplication from different angles, and repeated addition is only one of them. Alternatively, you can think of a number as the *operator* each time, acting on a succession of numbers from 1 to 12.

For example, the idea of repeated addition means that you construct your 2s table by saying '1 two is 2, 2 twos are 4, 3 twos are 6', etc. Or, you could recognize that 2 operates on other numbers *by doubling them*. This way you say the 2 first, and double the number being multiplied. So '2 ones are 2, 2 twos are 4, 2 threes are 6', etc. The advantage of this method is that you can work out '2 sevens' immediately, without having to recite the rest of the table first: you simply double seven, and there is your answer straightaway.

The only thing you have to be good at is doubling in your head, which is well within reach, even if it does take practice. There are two distinct procedures. One is adding numbers when the answer is less than ten. Help a child to achieve this by using all kinds of physical objects, and then resorting to his fingers if necessary. (That is what his fingers are there for, and there is no shame in using them.) Quite soon, he will be able to reach the answer 'by mind'.

Mental addition is a bit more complicated when the units go past the 'ten barrier'. In that case, you split the second number to make the first number up to ten. E.g. when adding 7+7, you need a 3 to make the first 7 up to 10. That 3 comes from the second 7, leaving 4. So 7+7 = 1 ten and 4 units, which is 14. The same principle works when adding any two numbers taking you beyond the next ten. I call it 'split addition'.

All you need to know in order to perform split addition are the numbers that go together to make 10:

$$9+1=10$$
$$8+2=10$$
$$7+3=10$$
$$6+4=10$$
$$5+5=10$$

Now reverse the pairs. Start with 5+5 again.

4 is 1 *less* than 5, so pair it with 1 *more* than 5:
$$4+6=10$$
3 is 1 *less* than 4, so pair it with 1 *more* than 6:
$$3+7=10$$

2 is 1 *less* than 3, so pair it with 1 *more* than 7:
$$2+8=10$$

1 is 1 *less* than 2, so pair it with 1 *more* than 8:
$$1+9=10$$

Summarize your results:
$$5+5=10$$
$$4+6=10$$
$$3+7=10$$
$$2+8=10$$
$$1+9=10$$

And there you are. Nothing to it – but armed with this knowledge a child really will be able to calculate any multiplication, in any of his tables, in about three or four seconds. So spend a little time helping him to learn the above pairs of numbers until they come unhesitatingly.

After that, you work out the 2s by doubling the number each time. For the 4s, you double the number, then double it again; and for the 8s, you double the number, double it again, and double it again. So if you want to work out 8 sevens, double seven (14), double it again (28), and double it again (56).

(When doubling larger numbers in your head, it is a good idea to double the tens first, then the units, and add your answers together. E.g. 2x14: 2 tens = 20, plus 2 fours = 8. When doubling 28, double the 2 tens = 40, then the 8 = 16. Add your answers = 40+16 = 56.)

Focus on the 10s table next. It's surprising how many children, at secondary level, even if they can count in tens, do not know that putting a 0 at the end of a number automatically multiplies it by 10.

To pave the way for the 10s, I reinvent numbers with my pupil – and we get in a right old pickle. We are ancient Romans to begin with, making one stroke for 1, two for 2, three for 3, and four for 4. (You will still find four strokes for 4 on clocks that have Roman numerals.) Then we decide this is getting silly, and five is going to be a V shape, so there. Four is one less than five = IV, and six is one more = VI. Haha, maybe we've cracked it. Seven is VII, eight is VIII   but those ones are creeping back again, difficult to count when we've got too many. What are we going to do for ten, anyway? Well, V is five, so let's put two Vs end to end for ten, which is X. In that case nine can be IX.

We go on lurching forward, using a combination of letters and ones to represent the numbers that we need to write. L is fifty, C is one hundred, D is five hundred, and M is one thousand. MDCCCCLXXVIII means one thousand, five hundred and four more hundreds, fifty and two more tens, then five and three – or 1978 in our figures! (Imagine if you had been an ancient Roman doing maths – now that would have been a pain in the neck.)

But long before the Romans, people in India had the brilliant idea of using single signs for *all* the numbers up to nine, instead of several marks:

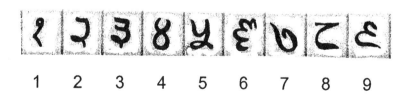

1   2   3   4   5   6   7   8   9

You can see that the signs for two and three have been made by joining two marks and three marks, but after that the signs bear no special relationship to the amount they represent. They are just arbitrary shapes.

This made it much easier to write and recognize numbers. (You didn't have to count the separate marks all the time.) But because numbers go on and on to infinity, inventing a single sign for every number would soon have been nearly as complicated as using separate marks.

Then one day, some lazy person was sitting down looking at his fingers, and realized that if you pressed all your fingers together, you could think of them as *one* bunch of ten. (All the best inventions have been thought of by lazy people who were trying to find short cuts...) So you could use the figure 1 to mean one unit, or one ten, by writing it in a different column:

Tens	Units
1	1

This means one ten, and one unit, and is a very useful way of writing 'eleven', in figures.

When you had ten bunches, you could put them all together in one heap, and use the same number '1' to mean one heap (or a hundred):

Hundreds	Tens	Units	
(10x10)	(10x1)	(1)	
1	1	1	One hundred and eleven

Ten heaps could be piled together to make a stack – or one thousand:

Thousands	Hundreds	Tens	Units	
(10x10x10)	(10x10)	(10x1)	(1)	One thousand,
1	1	1	1	one hundred and eleven

You could keep collecting in tens forever, by ruling up more columns.

You didn't even need to draw columns all the time.

Thousands	Hundreds	Tens	Units
2	7	5	4

meant 2 thousands, 7 hundreds, 5 tens (or 'fifty') and 4 units. But you could write 2754, without the lines, and it was every bit as obvious what that meant. The numbers had a value because of the *place* they were in – and every time you moved a number one *place* to the left, it got ten times bigger! (We call this a system of 'place value'.)

It worked well so long as you had a number in every (imaginary) column. Suppose, however, you wanted to write two thousand seven hundred and fifty, in figures. '275' means two *hundred* and seventy five – not what you want. You need a way of showing that there are *no units*.

If you draw a circle

starting at the top and going all the way round until you are back where you started, you get nowhere – so a circle is a very good shape for the idea of 'nothing'. *Now* you can show that a column is empty without having to draw the columns.

The number '275' means 'two hundred and seventy five'.

But '2750' means 'two thousand seven hundred and fifty', because the nought tells us there are no units. All the numbers to the left are therefore ten times bigger than they would be if the nought wasn't there.

And that is why putting a nought at the end multiplies a number by ten!

(Our numerals are called Arabic numerals, because they came from the Arabs, who learned them from the Indians. The numbers have changed a little in shape over the centuries, but the basic idea is the same.)

Once your pupil is familiar with the idea of place value, you can press on to decimal fractions. Numbers get ten times bigger every time they move one space to the left – and this goes on forever. In the same way, numbers get ten times smaller every time they move one space to the right; and this too can go on forever. Numbers to the right of the units column represent amounts that are less than one. The first column shows tenths, the next hundredths, the next thousandths, and so on. If you want to indicate this without drawing columns, you put a decimal point right after the units: 2754.3.

This decimal point *holds the place* of the units, so they cannot move even if you write a nought at the end of the number. (2754.30 means exactly the same as 2754.3.) Now if you want to make the number ten times bigger, by moving the figures to the left, you have to move the decimal point *one place to the right*: 27543.

So you multiply by ten by moving the decimal point to the right; you divide by ten by moving the decimal point to the left.

All this is preparation for a quick way of multiplying by five! Most children can count in fives, so reciting their 5s table is relatively easy; but they might still find it difficult to think of 'seven fives' straight off, without counting.

Because five is half of ten, halve the number you are multiplying, using decimal fractions if need be, then multiply by ten. E.g. half of 7 is 3.5 – multiply by 10 (move the decimal point one space to the right) = 35. So 5x7 = 35. You will get the same result if you multiply by ten first, and halve your answer (10x7 = 70, 70÷2 = 35) – let your child decide which he would rather do.

You are using easy tables as stepping-stones to the more difficult ones. The 2s lead on to the 4s and the 8s (doubling): the 10s lead on to the 5s (halving). Another easy table is the 11s – up to 11x9 you write the multiplied number twice (11x7 = 77). For 11x10 you write 11 followed by 0 (110), and then it isn't too difficult to add on another couple of elevens for 11x11 and 11x12.

And now your 12s are as easy as falling off a log. Multiply the number by 11, and add one more of the number to give you 12 of them. E.g. 11x7 = 77. 12x7 = 77+7 = 84 (use split addition).

This is the third and last procedure: I call it '1 away from' an easy table. The 12s are 1 away from the 11s; the 3s are 1 away from the 2s; and the 6s are 1 away from the 5s. So for 3x7, for example, you double the 7 (14), and add on another 7 (21).

The 9s are also 1 away from the 10s (in the other direction), but an even better way of working out your 9s is to use your fingers.

Spread all your fingers (and thumbs) on the table in front of you. If you want to work out 9x3, fold down your third finger, counting from the left:

The number of digits (fingers or thumbs) to the *left* of the finger you have folded down tells you the number of tens in your answer. The number of unfolded digits to the *right* tells you the number of units.

9x3 = 2 tens and 7 units = 27.

Try this with the other numbers in the 9s table – it always works, but only with the 9s.

So we have three easy tables (2s, 10s, 11s) and three procedures: **doubling** (2s, 4s, 8s); **halving** (5s); and **1 away** (12s, 3s, 6s, 9s). [Note that '1 away' means '1 more or less than', not that you are taking away...] Surprisingly, that covers all your tables except one: the 7s.

When I reached this point I couldn't think of a nice neat procedure for the 7s – and then I realized I didn't have to.

Because there are procedures for all the other tables, the 7s can be worked out using those other tables. And, this is an excellent way of reviewing all the procedures.

Here is the 7s table:

7s
(Use your other tables)

$1x7 = 7$
$2x7 = 7+7 = 14$ *doubling*
$3x7 = 14+7 = 21$ *1 away (2s)*
$4x7 = 14+14 = 28$ *doubling*
$5x7 = 70÷2 = 35$ *halving*
$6x7 = 35+7 = 42$ *1 away (5s)*
$7x7 = 49$
$8x7 = 28+28 = 56$ *doubling*
$9x7 = 70-7 = 63$ *1 away (10s); fingers*
$10x7 = 70$ *easy*
$11x7 = 77$ *easy*
$12x7 = 77+7 = 84$ *1 away (11s)*

Well yes, your child does have to learn that $7x7 = 49$. But I expect he can manage that.

(My next project is a little booklet called *Know Your Multiplication Tables – without having to learn them,* which explains the above procedures in more detail. Watch this space.)

The aim of working out the tables in the way I have described is twofold. Your child is really engaging with numbers, from the inside, at every step of the way, which is very empowering. Secondly, he can go straight to the answers, without reciting at all.

So, of course, they are his 'straight-there' tables…

VI

Tackling the confusion

The Davis Solution

Brain Gym

Colour it clear

The 'ways around the blockages' are a good idea because your child knows she can use them to get where she wants to go. There are no nasty surprises lurking in the undergrowth, waiting for an opportunity to trip her up.

You can offer them with assurance because they will help *any* child to understand print, read aloud, spell correctly, write creatively and neatly, tell the time, and learn the alphabet, days of the week, months of the year, historical dates, and multiplication tables. So long as you are always supportive and encouraging, you cannot go wrong.

They don't cure the confusion, however. The perceptual problem(s) are still there, making your child's life more of an uphill struggle, in other areas, than it needs to be. Is it possible to tackle the confusion head on, and get rid of it altogether – or at least put your child in control, so she can recognize and deal with it whenever she needs to?

It may be.

The Davis solution: re-positioning the 'mind's eye'

The first perceptual problem is Orton's 'strephosymbolia', or 'twisted symbols', caused by a confusion of images recorded on both sides of the brain. This phenomenon is also what lies behind the *gift* of dyslexia, because it often results in the ability to visualize in three dimensions. (See Chapter IV.)

Ron Davis, in his book *The Gift of Dyslexia,* describes the ability from a different perspective. As far as he is concerned, the child is always the one in control, (although she may not consciously realize it), because she can move her mental eye around an object at will. She discovers how to do this in early childhood, when it is a brilliant way of resolving confusion. Disaster strikes when she goes to school and tries to do it with written words and numbers, etc., and it doesn't resolve the confusion, but compounds it.

However, as Davis points out, if the child is the one causing the confusion, however subconsciously, *she can learn how not to do it*. She herself can learn how to hold her mental eye still, so that she can visualize words and numbers nice and flat, the way they appear to everybody else.

When the mind's eye is roving freely, Davis calls the resulting confusion 'disorientation'. He hit upon this explanation for his own difficulties as a result of trying to write about his sculpting technique for a fellow sculptor. He focused all his energies on trying to encapsulate that creative process in words; but hours later, when he attempted to re-read what he had written, he discovered that his letter was a bunch of meaningless scrawls, and totally illegible.

Could it be, Davis wondered later, that when he was at his most creative, he was also at his most dyslexic – that a way of seeing, mentally, which informed his artistic talent, was the very same mode of perception which played havoc with his spelling? If so, he reasoned – if his dyslexia could be changed by something he was doing mentally – it could not possibly be a structural problem, but must be a functional problem. *And that meant there had to be something he could do about it.*

Three days later, he worked out how to correct his perceptual distortions. Then he went to the library, picked up *Treasure Island,* and, for the first time in his life, read a book from cover to cover in a few hours.

After that, he could not possibly keep such a discovery to himself. He developed a way of showing fellow sufferers how to resolve their own perceptual distortions: and even better, of training others to carry out the same procedure with struggling dyslexics. His work has achieved solid and quite spectacular results – when a Davis Orientation Counselling session is correctly performed, it produces a 97 per cent success rate. To cap it all, Davis has described and illustrated the procedure so clearly in his book that anyone can do it. If you suspect that someone you love may be battling with dyslexia, this book is an absolute must.

Being able to reposition her mind's eye means that a child really can have the best of both worlds. She can still send it spinning off whenever her creative side is at full throttle: but keep it on a short leash when she needs to focus on printed shapes.

I do part company with Davis, though, in the area of literacy teaching methods. He doesn't seem to be familiar with Susanne Langer, so lacks her insight into the ways that spoken language is understood; nor has he come across Doman's comparison between written language and spoken language (see Chapters II and III.) He misses the crucial idea that word recognition depends on matching the perceived word (spoken or written) with some form of the word in the head, and why this can be especially problematical for dyslexics learning to read and spell. He assumes (like a great many literacy teachers) that learning to read is a matter of performance; so when a child stumbles over particular words, this triggers disorientation, and aggravates her distress. Davis therefore lists all these 'trigger words', and suggests ways of teaching them, individually, at some length.

As soon as you abandon the idea that a youngster learning to read has to pull herself up by her own bootstraps and work it all out for herself, teaching any child to read becomes easy and straightforward. You give her massive experience of understanding print by encouraging her to look at the text while you read to her; and massive experience of sounding out written words by doing it for her and with her until she can do it on her own. So she never has to cope unaided with Davis' 'trigger words' before they have become familiar friends, at which point she can take them in her stride without worrying about them.

That said, however, Davis' way of teaching the alphabet, by helping a child to make both lower case and upper case versions in clay, seems excellent; likewise his approach to punctuation, and what he calls 'spell-reading'. I would suggest that you follow my ideas about teaching reading, phonics and spelling, but keep Davis' methods on spell-reading etc. up your sleeve for use with any child who seems to need 'a bit extra' for complete mastery.

Physical solutions: Brain Gym

Davis' work, combined with Orton's, is exciting and positive, because it makes clear that dyslexia is in no way an intellectual shortcoming. (Quite the reverse.) The condition is much more like a physical handicap than a mental one, and its origins are perceptual. It is as if a child really needs to be wearing a pair of inner spectacles in order to see straight, but no one has supplied them because no one has realized what is going wrong, or how to put it right. When a child has to wear ordinary glasses, we would never dream of calling her stupid or lazy if she struggles to read and write without them: it is equally inappropriate to use such terms when the missing glasses are intangible!

Because these perceptual problems are themselves rooted in the physical confusion of images between the left and right side of the brain, it makes sense to assume that there could well be physical solutions to the physical difficulty. And, indeed, there are. Once Davis has enabled his students to reposition their mind's eye, he goes on to help them address the problem of coordination by catching balls in either hand while balancing on one foot or the other.

Another programme offering a physical solution is Brain Gym, developed by Dr Paul Dennison in the late sixties. Like Davis, Dennison was severely dyslexic himself, and intrigued by the connection between physical activity and learning ability. He experimented with ways to make reading easier for himself, and devised a series of exercises that he taught children at his first clinic in 1969. They were used mainly to assist those with disabilities such as dyslexia, dyspraxia, autism and attention deficit disorder (hyperactivity), and were later extended to 'normal' children.

The exercises are specifically designed to help the two sides of the brain work together better. Here are instructions for some of them:

Cross Crawl

While standing, lift your right knee and touch it with your left hand, then lift your left knee and touch it with your right hand. Repeat 10 to 15 times. Helps with: reading, writing, listening, memory and co-ordination.

Brain Buttons

Make a U-shape with the thumb and index finger of one hand and place in the centre of your chest just below your collar bone. Gently rub this acupressure point for 20 or 30 seconds while placing your other hand over your navel. Then change hands and repeat. Helps with: clear thinking, keeping pace while reading and focus.

Hook-ups

While sitting or standing, cross one ankle over the other. Cross the same-side wrist over the other and touch palms together, thumbs downwards. Interlace fingers and draw hands up towards the chest. Rest your tongue on the roof of your mouth so your jaw relaxes. Sit or stand this way for one minute, eyes closed, breathing deeply. Then change your feet and hands around and cross them the other way. Helps with: stress, self-esteem and listening.

Lazy Eights

Extend one arm in front. With one thumb pointing upwards, slowly and smoothly trace a large figure eight on its side in the air. Keep your neck relaxed and your head upright, moving only slightly as you focus on the thumb and follow it around. Helps with: reading, writing and hand-eye coordination.

The Elephant

Place the left ear on the left shoulder, extend the left arm like the trunk of an elephant and, with knees relaxed, use your outstretched hand to draw a lying-down eight sign, starting from the middle and moving the hand upwards to draw the left 'bulge' of the eight first. Look down your arm at your hand while you're doing it. Switch arms after three to five signs. Helps with: hand-eye coordination and focus.

Several schools have now included a Brain Gym programme, as part of their school day, for all pupils – and have noted dramatic improvements as a result. For example, Brain Gym is used by pupils aged from four to nine at Balliol Lower School in Kempsford, Bedfordshire, who do their exercises three times a day – when they arrive in the morning, after break and after lunch. Children are also encouraged to bring in a water bottle to sip from whenever they want, because drinking water throughout the day has been proved to increase alertness. Head teacher Lisa Scott says: "There's a lot of social deprivation in the area and children were coming to school worrying about what was happening at home. The exercises calm them. We've been doing Brain Gym for three years and it's part of school life now. The children do the exercises if they're feeling tired or having difficulty concentrating. Whether it's psychological or whether it works on a deeper level I don't know, but it works. With the brighter pupils it gives them a sharper focus and puts them in the right learning mode." Other schools report similar findings.

Dr Dennison has written several books, including *Brain Gym* and *Brain Gym for Teachers*. For more information, and details of national events, teachers and courses, contact: Edu-K Foundation UK, 12 Golders Rise, Hendon, London NW4 2HR. Tel: 020 8202 3141. See also Carla Hannaford's *Smart Moves: Why Learning Is Not All In Your Head*, for a study of Brain Gym.

The Irlen solution: colour it clear

Nowhere in his book does Ron Davis refer to Helen Irlen's work (see Chapter IV); so maybe he has never come across it. This is a pity, because Scotopic Sensitivity (Irlen) Syndrome is a most significant piece in the jigsaw puzzle of dyslexia, and the Irlen solution can resolve several apparently intractable problems for dyslexia sufferers.

But it can do more. Coloured glasses help not only with reading and writing, but also in fields that seem quite unrelated to literacy. Children who are keen on ball games find that with their new spectacles they can suddenly see the ball more sharply and clearly; and autistic youngsters have discovered that many of their compulsive behaviours (like head banging etc.) melt away when they view the world through coloured lenses. (One explanation for this is that the filters screen out a significant amount of sensory bombardment which previously made their lives unbearable.) Hyperactive children become calmer and more focused. So all teachers need to be aware of the great benefits, for some children, of looking out at life through tinted spectacles.

The snag is that an Irlen consultation doesn't come cheap, and the glasses can cost upwards of £200. However, there are inexpensive alternatives, at least to begin with. I used to screen whole classes of children at once, with theatrical gels instead of the proper Irlen overlays. (Irlen herself used these in the early stages of her work.) This gives you a pretty good indication of the pupils who may benefit from further investigation.

The following colours seem to cover most children's needs: Rosco 10, Medium yellow; Rosco 33, Pink; Rosco 55, Lilac; Rosco 63, Pale blue; Rosco 96, Lime; Rosco 388, Gaslight Green; Lee 024, Scarlet; Lee 101, Yellow; Lee 116, Medium blue green; Lee 213, White flame green. The gels come in large sheets which can be cut up into page sized overlays, 20cm by 12cm – 12 overlays from a Rosco sheet, and 24 from a Lee sheet. You can order them direct from Stage Electrics, Cofton Road, Marsh

Barton, Exeter EX2 8QW. Tel: 01392 55868. Or there may be a local store nearer to hand – consult the Yellow Pages.

Use enlarged copies of the scoring chart (see next page) to help children decide if the coloured gels make a difference when used as overlays for reading; and if so, which ones are the most helpful. Pass round 'testers', and ask each pupil to give the gels a score from 1-10, depending on how much difference they make. Offer dictionaries with fairly small print to test the gels, so the child isn't trying to read the page, just responding to the look of the print. The overlays should be placed across half a page, then the two halves can be compared. You can intensify a colour by using one sheet on top of another, or combine different colours in the same way.

In class, it helps to have a supply of assorted gels for the children to borrow when reading. Also, photocopy worksheets in a variety of colours, and allow pupils to write on coloured paper, or in coloured pens, if this makes a difference. Many children prefer using different coloured fonts for computer work, on shaded backgrounds. Ask your students if they find it easier to read writing on whiteboards in certain colours, and to remind you if you forget! When this approach is adopted, as a matter of course, for all children, nobody should feel singled out, or that they are struggling to read text in colours that they cannot see.

If overlays prove helpful, it is likely that coloured glasses will be even more so. Irlen Syndrome does not show up on conventional eye tests, and must be detected by qualified practitioners. However, some local authorities are now providing this service – check and find out. But it may well be quicker and cheaper in the long run to obtain genuine Irlen overlays and/or glasses. Information and advice is available from Patricia Clayton, West Country Irlen Centre, 123 High Street, Chard, Somerset TA20 1QT. Tel: 01460 65555.

NAME_____

SCOTOPIC SENSITIVITY (IRLEN) SYNDROME – SCORING CHART FOR THEATRICAL GELS

Coloured gel	Helps	How much? 1-10
ROSCO		
Medium Yellow (10)		
Pink (33)		
Lilac (55)		
Pale blue (63)		
Lime (96)		
Gaslight green (388)		
LEE		
Scarlet (024)		
Yellow (101)		
Medium Blue Green (116)		
White flame green (213)		
List colours required.	Say if you want 1 or 2 of each	

VII

Why are schools getting it wrong — and how can they get it right?

Total literacy for all children

Once we have seen that written language really does work exactly like spoken language, we can raise our expectations, for all children, quite dramatically. There is no reason why any child should not be fully literate by the time he or she leaves school; and in fact this goal can be reached during the first couple of years at primary school with no trouble at all.

By 'fully literate', I mean that a child should be able to read and understand any material that is at his interest level; he should be able to read it aloud, unaided, easily and fluently; and he should be able to write or type anything he wants to, making sure that his work is legible, and correctly spelled and punctuated.

Written language is a tool, not an end in itself. Children who can read have access to anything that has ever been thought and written down. Children who can write can convey their own ideas to a much wider audience than is possible when they can only talk. So when all children are fully literate, schools can get on with their real job of helping youngsters to explore the whole vast expanse of human achievement.

As we aim at total literacy, for all children, very early on, we are greatly helped by the recognition that there are two quite distinct 'reading' processes. One is seeing meanings in written words (understanding print); and the other is being able to match written words with spoken words (reading aloud). Either process can operate without any necessary reference to the other one. All children need to be adept at both processes (rather than one or the other) – so we must ensure that this happens, for all children.

Pistols at dawn – the great literacy debate

Unfortunately, as far as literacy teaching methods are concerned, the twentieth century has been a vast battlefield. The opposing armies have championed one process or the other, passionately maintaining that only *their* process is the right way to teach reading, and giving short shrift to everything else.

Up to 1945, most schools in the UK used a phonic 'method'. Children learned their letters first, then how to put them together to make words, then how to follow the print from left to right; then, finally, they were allowed to read books – which all had to be phonically regular at first.

But many educationists were growing dubious about this approach. They had discovered that it was quite possible to recognize words as wholes, even if you didn't know the individual letters, and this enabled children to read less stilted material, much sooner. They called their method 'look-and-say': you looked at a word while the teacher said it, then you said it yourself and practised it quite a bit, after which you were supposed to be able to recognize it whenever you encountered it. You worked your way through a 'look-and-say' reading scheme, gradually moving on to 'proper' books in the fullness of time. Phonics was taught incidentally, as an aid to word recognition, nothing more – and if you could manage without it, so much the better.

Most of the 'look-and-say' readers were still pretty silly, however, because of the need for a controlled vocabulary, and frequent repetition. Text like 'Here is Peter. Here is Jane. Look at the ball. The dog has the ball,' hardly qualifies as deathless prose, and was brilliantly satirized by Wendy Cope in her poem about the milkman having an affair with Mummy while Daddy was at work: 'Daddy looks very cross. Has he a gun? Up milkman! Up milkman! Over the wall! Here is Peter. Here is Jane. They like fun. Look, Jane, look! Look at the dog! See him run!'

'Look-and-say' could be called a 'whole word' approach: in the seventies and eighties, teachers began to move towards a 'whole *language*' approach. The idea was that single words made sense only in the context of complete sentences; and the sentences themselves should be read in the context of a still larger whole. The artificial language of reading schemes was abandoned in favour of the much more natural language of 'real books'; again, phonics played a minimal part in the proceedings.

1985 saw the publication of Liz Waterland's *Read With Me: An Apprenticeship Approach to Reading*. Waterland was the deputy head of Brewster Avenue Infant School, Peterborough. Supported by her head teacher, she threw out the reading schemes, and furnished her classroom with all the most tempting, irresistible books she could find, by the best children's authors, crammed with luscious illustrations, and just begging to be taken off the shelves and devoured. A child or couple of children would choose a book, and Liz would read it to them, snuggled up on a sofa, while they marvelled at the pictures. 'This is Hannah, aged four,' reports Liz in *Read With Me,* 'who brought *Fat Cat* to me for four days running, each day needing less help. "I'll read it all tomorrow," she said. And did. What a Friday!' Parents and other volunteers were invited to take part in the classroom and at home. The approach spread like wildfire: *Read With Me* sold in its thousands.

All this is good stuff, and is the best way of helping children to understand print that has ever been devised. Hannah was following the print while Liz read it to her, so she was learning to recognize the words at considerable speed. There was abundant repetition of the book's vocabulary, in an entirely meaningful context; and it isn't surprising that, by Friday, Hannah could read *Fat Cat* aloud on her own.

The trouble is that Waterland's approach was based on the work of two specialists in linguistics, Kenneth Goodman (*Reading – a Psycholinguistic Guessing Game,* 1967) and Frank Smith (*Understanding Reading,* 1971, and *Reading,* 1978). Their work took the educational world by storm from the sixties onwards. And it has to be said that the language theory of these two thinkers is deeply flawed.

For example, Frank Smith declares in his book *Reading*: 'reading makes no demands that the brain does not meet in the comprehension of speech' – exactly what Doman had been maintaining some years before, that understanding print is comparable to understanding speech. (See Chapter III.) But Smith goes on to assume from this that sentences give meaning to the words they contain, rather than vice versa. He thinks his conclusion is proved by research showing that people read material such as EARLY FROSTS HARM THE CROPS more speedily than they can read five unrelated words, e.g. SNEEZE FURY HORSES WHEN AGAIN. So children learn to understand written sentences by *predicting* what is coming next, on the basis of what they have already read.

Even the most cursory examination of how we understand spoken language demonstrates that this is simply not the case. Take the very sentence that Smith mentions: 'Early frosts harm the crops'. Imagine you are listening to someone saying it, and they stop at the word 'harm'. What comes next? Haven't the foggiest, have you! It *could* be 'the crops'; or it could be 'pensioners'; or 'the tourist industry'; or even 'wild animals that collect food for the winter'. You have no way of knowing what is going to be harmed by these early frosts until the speaker completes his sentence. Then you do; because you recognize and understand each individual word that follows 'harm'.

Smith and Goodman have made an elementary blunder. They have confused the meanings of the words in a sentence with their grammatical function. You can certainly predict that what comes after 'harm' is likely to be a direct object of the verb, because you are so familiar with the grammatical structure of English sentences. But you cannot possibly identify the meaning of that direct object until you have heard what the speaker has to say.

Of course this is as it should be. Language exists to tell us things we did not know before. If we could really predict how sentences were going to turn out, then we wouldn't need language in the first place, and we might as well all pack up and go home.

Sadly, Smith's disciples have elevated his ideas into a theory of teaching practice. Children should be encouraged to guess unfamiliar written words by thinking of the meaning of what has preceded them; and if their guesses are only approximate, this doesn't matter so long as they 'make sense'.

The resulting 'whole language' philosophy is rooted in a much more ancient assumption, virtually endemic in teaching theory, which is that learning to read is a matter of performance. Children have to be *doing* something in order to demonstrate what they have learned, or are learning. They have to be saying their letters; or sounding out written words without help; or saying whole words in response to flash cards; or, finally, 'guessing' or 'predicting' the meanings of words. We could call it the 'academic' approach; and it can be extraordinarily difficult for many teachers – and parents – to adopt other ways of thinking. (I had similar difficulty when I began my journey of exploration.)

The 'experience' approach

We just have to keep reminding ourselves how children learn spoken language, as I described in Chapter II. We would never dream of 'testing' babies learning to hear language, or worry about how well they are 'doing'. No, we barrel on regardless, flooding them in a veritable sea of spoken words, phrases, suggestions, instructions and descriptions, all of which refer to an immediate physical reality, (real or imagined), which supplies the meaning of what they are hearing. The same is true when they are learning to talk. We imitate the sounds a baby produces, so encouraging him to go on making them; we say words very slowly and clearly when we realize a baby wants to say them himself; if he makes a mistake, we tend to be thrilled that he is trying at all, and then repeat the word correctly. "Oh, clever you – yes, that's a ba-na-na, isn't it."

We could call this an 'experience' approach (as opposed to an 'academic' one). All the time we are giving a child the continual experience of success, so it never even occurs to him to suppose that failure is possible. And there is no doubt that it works – millions and millions of children, worldwide, learn their mother tongue very well indeed through the 'experience' approach.

It is as easy to use an 'experience' approach when we are teaching children to read and write, as I have found out. We surround them with the plenteous experience of meaningful written language – labels on objects, posters, road signs, headlines in newspapers, word cards, the text in books that we read to them. All the time we keep on telling them what the words mean, eliciting a response every now and then by asking "Show me the word that says..." After a while we provide the supported experience of reading running text aloud, gently correcting them if they make a mistake. We don't ask them to 'guess' or 'predict', only absorb. When it comes to sounding out words, we tell them the whole word first, then demonstrate how to match it with the equivalent sounds, until they can manage that process, too, by themselves. The same delightfully relaxed way of teaching can be extended to writing, spelling, typing – any of the literacy skills that we want them to acquire.

I dubbed it the 'bicycle' approach when I was helping my daughters to read and write. There are two possible ways of teaching a child to ride a bicycle. You can show him the bicycle, supplying names for the wheels, pedals, handlebars, saddle, etc., and explaining how the pedals operate the wheels. After that, it's up to him. Alternatively, you can sit him on the machine, place his hands firmly on the handlebars, and hold the bicycle steady while you push it along, and he has the feeling of his feet going round on the pedals. Some time later, you let go of the handlebars and just hold the saddle. Then one day, when he isn't looking, you let go of the saddle as well – and he realizes that he can ride the bicycle all by himself.

Method A may be good for his soul (although even that is doubtful); but if what you want him to be able to do is to ride a bike, you will go for Method B every time.

I decided that I wasn't interested in making my daughters work out how to decipher written language without much help. My goal was for them to be able to read and write anything they wanted to, as quickly as possible. So I gave them the abundant experience of doing exactly that; and in no time at all they were riding off into the distance with the wind in their hair and broad grins all over their faces.

Another analogy that I use in my work with parents is to describe written language as an enchanted kingdom, set in the middle of an island, surrounded by a marsh. You have an unlimited supply of planks, but although they are as long as the marsh is wide, they are not quite long enough to rest on its shores. No matter: you keep dropping the planks into the marsh, from shore to shore, one at a time, on top of each other. They all disappear, and no one except you knows they are there. But quite unseen, the pile of planks continues to rise steadily to the top of the marsh, until one day the topmost plank is level with the surface; and your child can walk across without even getting his feet muddy!

Your job is to continue dropping the planks – and it does take courage, particularly when nothing much seems to be happening. But screw your courage to the sticking place – keep on and on and on providing the experience – and as long as you have made sure that your child can see the words, he cannot help but learn, because that is how his brain works. Trust him, and yourself. You taught him spoken language, didn't you – so you know that you are a brilliant teacher, and he is a brilliant learner.

Although Liz Waterland may have been bamboozled by her studies into paying lip service to 'whole language' theory, her practice is far superior, because it focuses on this huge provision of meaningful experience. That is why she describes her way of working as an apprenticeship approach. However, with respect to reading, even the term 'apprenticeship' doesn't quite hit the nail on the head. It implies that you are showing a child how to do something; and after a while, he will be able to do it by himself. But reading to a child while he follows the print is even more powerful than that. You are not showing him how to read, you are giving him the direct experience of understanding written language right then and there, because he is looking at the words and seeing their meanings while you read. So calling it the 'experience' approach is probably clearest and best.

'Whole language' and phonics

When it comes to phonics teaching, though, Waterland has definitely been led astray by her mentors. Frank Smith devotes quite a large section of his book on *Reading* to 'the fallacy of phonics', with the result that virtually all 'whole language' teachers, including Waterland, insist that it isn't necessary to teach phonics in the early stages of reading at all.

But Smith's pronouncements about phonics are very muddled. He supposes that you have to learn phonics by memorizing hundreds of different spelling-to-sound correspondences – and then you must set to work to learn all the exceptions. He thinks that the only purpose of phonics is to enable a reader to discover the meaning of an unfamiliar word by sounding it out – and rejects the procedure because it doesn't work every time. (E.g. you cannot tell the difference between the sounds for the words 'horse' and 'horizon' by using phonics, only if you already know what they say.) Finally, although he recognizes that understanding print is a process in its own right, he doesn't distinguish nearly carefully enough between seeing meanings in written words, and being able to match them with sounds.

This is such an important distinction that it is well worth clarifying. Two simple examples will suffice. Imagine you are a small deaf child, reading the following sentence. You don't know how to say the words, or even what they sound like, but when you look at them you see quite clearly what they mean:

The chocolate fudge is in a jar on the top shelf in the kitchen.

You have learned to understand written language in the same way that a hearing child learns to understand speech. (This has been achieved in practice. Back in the twenties, Dr Helen Thompson developed a way of teaching profoundly deaf children to understand print by presenting written words in a physical context. Words such as 'go', 'jump' and 'run' were shown to the children, accompanied by the relevant actions, as well as nouns like 'table', 'door', 'window' and so on. Then the teachers would hold up sentences – e.g. 'Go to your table' – demonstrating the action required, until the children could carry out the actions in response to the written instructions. The children had no difficulty learning to read in this way, and at the end of a year had achieved 5/6 of the comprehension standard of a normal hearing class.)

You could prove that you have understood the sentence by dragging a chair into the kitchen, climbing up, and helping yourself to the fudge.

Now have a look at another sentence, written in Swahili:

Siku ya kwanza alileta mayai kumi na matano; siku ya pili, kumi na sita; na siku ya tatu, kumi.

(If you can understand Swahili, pretend you can't.) The Swahili written language is totally phonetic, but one or two sound values are different from ours. The letter 'i' is pronounced 'ee', 'ay' and 'ai' are both pronounced 'ī', and 'e' is pronounced 'ā'. Armed with this information, you could scrutinize each word and read the sentence aloud. But if I said to you, "Oh well done, you have read that beautifully," you would give me a disgusted look. "Do me a favour," you would say. "I haven't read it at all. I don't have the remotest idea what it's about."

You are right, you haven't read it. What you have done with it has been valid, satisfying and useful – it just isn't reading. Notice also that the way you look at the two sentences is quite different. When you read the first sentence, you see the words as transparent wholes, and you have the feeling of looking through them. When you tackle the second sentence, your focal point comes sharply forward. Instead of looking through the words, you look at them, much more analytically. Now your intention is to separate the words into bits, so as to match sounds to each bit, and produce an equivalent spoken version.

The interesting thing is that when you read normally, your brain is operating both (apparently contradictory) processes simultaneously! If you are engrossed in a book, your main concern is with the meaning of what you are reading, and you are busily constructing all kinds of mental pictures which reflect the unfolding story. Nevertheless, your brain is also aware of the matching spoken words, in detail; and if you want to, you can slow down and 'hear' the words you are reading.

The ideal is for all children to be able to read like you, and operate both processes at the same time without even thinking about it. But it makes sense, at first, to teach them separately, and then encourage a youngster to combine them as soon as he can.

The first process is 'real reading' – looking at a written text and seeing the meanings through the words (just as 'real hearing' is a matter of listening to someone talking and also 'hearing the meanings' through the words). Matching written words with spoken words is not reading at all, but is an enormously powerful aid to reading – and to hearing – and to speaking – and to spelling – because it makes possible the rapid transfer of meaning from speech to print, or from print to speech.

You don't have to memorize hundreds of different spelling-to-sound correspondences, plus all the exceptions, in order to learn phonics. On the contrary, you learn one straightforward technique, in three steps: first sound onto left-hand edge; match the ends and middles; blend the sounds as you go along, working from beginning to end. The technique is the same for all words, no matter how irregular. E.g. in a word like 'knife', the 'n' sound maps onto the 'kn', and the 'f' sound maps onto the 'fe' – this is why thinking of the 'edges' of a written word, rather than the 'first letter' or the 'last letter' is helpful. I call it the 'tallying' approach to phonics, because that is exactly what you are doing – you are tallying sounds with shapes, right the way along both words, until they are firmly matched in every detail.

When you use the tallying approach, no child is expected to match written words with spoken words by himself before he has had a great deal of practice in doing so with help. Reading aloud to him while he looks at the words is the first stage, because he is not only seeing the meanings of the words while you read, he is also thinking of the matching spoken words at the same time. Then you enable him to map written and spoken words onto each other bit by bit, until he can operate that process as well, independently.

By this time he will be able to read aloud any unfamiliar, regular words without hesitation; and manage those with only slight peculiarities by using context clues. (Notice that 'using context clues' is not a matter of 'guessing' or 'predicting', but of logical *deduction*, which is very different. It mirrors the identical way that a baby establishes the meanings of new spoken words.

For example, suppose a baby's mother says to him, "Let's put your red trousers on today," while she is wriggling the garment over his legs. Some time later she remarks, "Here's your red fire engine – it was under the chair!" and still later, "Let's look at your big red book – I like the pictures in that." The baby observes that the same pattern of sounds – 'red' – occurs in the three sentences; so there must be something the same about all three objects. Well, they share the same bright colour – so the baby deduces that is the meaning of the word 'red'. Further experience confirms his initial deduction. Your fledgling reader can operate the same process.) He will probably need you to keep on telling him oddities such as 'laugh' or 'shoulder' for a little while, though.

In addition, he can transfer words from his reading vocabulary to his hearing and speaking vocabularies by sounding them out, and remember how to spell them by thinking of their matching sounds. (See Chapter V.)

Launching a child into the world of written language by helping him only to understand print is like sending him into battle with one arm tied behind his back; so why on earth limit him in this way?

Edward's story

It is important to make sure that all children can see the matching sounds for written words, as well as their meanings, from the very earliest stages of learning to read. Otherwise it is quite possible for a child to forge ahead with 'real reading', without being able to read aloud at all. I learned this to my cost when I was working with Edward, a twelve-year-old dyslexic whose reading and spelling levels, on entry to secondary education, were virtually non-existent.

I taught him systematic phonics, very rapidly (his primary school hadn't bothered), and then went for abundant exposure to meaningful written language, reading to him as much as I could, both at home and at school, holding the book so he could follow the print. The books were always Edward's choice, and at his interest level – *The Midnight Adventure* by Raymond Briggs, then *Charlie and the Chocolate Factory* and *The BFG* by Roald Dahl. I would read a couple of chapters, and Edward read back a paragraph or so that I had just finished, sounding out any words which presented difficulties. Then Edward re-read everything we had covered, by himself, before the next session.

Things began to gather momentum as we pressed ahead with *Charlie and the Chocolate Factory*. "Where did we get to, Edward?" I said once, early on into the book. "Here, Miss," he declared, finding the page straightaway. There was a small pause; I felt an undercurrent of excitement in the air. Then, triumphantly, "But *I* have got to here," turning over a flurry of pages, and trying not to grin as he looked up at me. "Oh Edward, that's amazing, that's a whole chapter, tell me about it." So he did.

We started *The BFG*, and almost immediately Edward was away for two weeks. This was a frequent occurrence, and I began to feel that we would never make up the lost time. But the next time I saw Edward he was jubilant, and informed me excitedly that he had finished the whole book (except for the last page). "Edward, that's fantastic, you only started it two weeks ago. Tell me about it." So he did: Sophie being kidnapped by the Big Friendly Giant, all the other horrible giants, collecting the dreams, visiting the Queen, and the final rout of the man-eaters. The Queen, he informed me, lived in the House of Commons, but he was quite happy to alter that to Buckingham Palace when I explained. "I knew it was somewhere important, Miss."

(This was long before the video was available – there was no way that Edward could have discovered the story, other than by reading the book, just as he said he had.)

But when I asked him to read aloud the final page, *he couldn't do it*. Every fourth or fifth word was a battle, even though I had read the page to him two minutes previously. The weird thing was that when I reminded him to sound out words he didn't know, he could do that quite easily, in a surprised 'Oh yes' tone of voice, as if he was chiding himself for not having thought of doing it before. It clearly didn't occur to him to use the procedure when he was reading on his own.

He read the rest of the Roald Dahls, *A Game of Soldiers* by Jan Needle (an ordinary little paperback about the Falklands war) and embarked on Tolkien, taking possession of *The Hobbit* with practised ease, and even tackling *The Lord of the Rings*. But he still found that reading aloud was an uphill struggle.

I wrote about Edward in various journals, and began to hear from other teachers who had encountered 'Edwards' of their own – children who could read and understand whole books, but were unable to read them aloud. So Edward was by no means an isolated instance.

However, I had short-changed Edward. Because he was focusing so intently on the meanings of the written words, without even thinking of the spoken version until I asked him to, he was not establishing the match between print and speech every time he read. He might have been able to consume Tolkien, but work sheets for Science or Humanities were a different matter, and his written work was still illegible because of his spelling. I realized it wasn't enough just to teach him phonics. I should have made sure that he practised reading aloud extensively, until the spoken words were coming out of his ears (and mouth), *before* he had completely free access to the world of literature. Then, as well as understanding the texts, he would also have been reading them aloud inside his head, like most of us, with all the advantages which that ability provides.

The three keys

There are three keys to achieving total literacy for every child, in the shortest possible time. The first is to use an experience approach, not an academic one: you go on supplying all the help necessary, right across the board, until each pupil is fully independent.

The second key is to provide ample experience, from the start, of both ways of operating on print: understanding written words, and matching them with sounds, in detail.

The third is what I call the 'as if' key. It will enable dyslexic pupils to learn reading and writing, in an ordinary classroom, almost as easily as their peers.

The existence of dyslexia has been recognized for many decades. There have always been these 'awkward' children who do not seem to make progress at school, and by and large the educational system has not known what to do about them, or even what to call the condition. It tends to take refuge in the term 'specific learning difficulty', which doesn't explain very much, and gets us no further forward on the practical front. The British Dyslexia Association, a charity, has done a valiant job in discovering ways of teaching dyslexic children, and offering support and reassurance to parents. Understandably, however, it has tended to focus on early identification coupled with separate provision – i.e. withdrawal from mainstream lessons, and an intensive programme of phonic drills, multisensory learning, special handwriting etc., plus in-class support as the youngsters grow older.

This is a lot better than nothing, but there are two serious disadvantages. One is that you will not succeed in identifying every struggler: many children inevitably fall through the net. The other is that extraction classes are rarely satisfactory. They are expensive because you have to pay for additional teachers (that's if you can find ones who understand dyslexia). And what lessons do you withdraw the children from, without further damaging their self-esteem, and their overall educational entitlement?

I believe that the solution is a good deal less complicated. The best ways of teaching dyslexics – the 'ways around the blockages' described in Chapter V – are really the best ways of teaching *all* children. All primary school children benefit from being read to, rapid systematic phonics, practising reading aloud, making clay alphabets, compiling a 'saying-for-spelling' vocabulary, using spelling dictionaries, cursive handwriting and typing skills, and learning by heart. So the way forward is to teach all children *as if any single child could be dyslexic.*

Then no child will fall through the net, you will be stopping literacy problems before they even begin – and you will save the money that might have been spent on extraction lessons.

It is useful to identify dyslexia at an early age, but you don't *have* to identify the dyslexics in a class in order to teach them properly. My philosophy now is to assume all children are dyslexic until they've proved they're not! It doesn't affect the way I teach them one iota. Why not do the same in every primary school classroom – and watch all the children flourish?

Revolution at Longniddry

There are schools in the UK which are doing precisely that. At the present time they seem to be mostly in Scotland, but I live in hope.

I first made contact with Longniddry Primary School, in East Lothian, through the pages of *Special Children* (a superb educational journal written for and about those with 'barriers to learning'). Chastened by my experience with Edward, I set to work to make it as easy as possible for other teachers to avoid my mistakes. So I designed a pack of phonic word cards which would teach the sounding-out technique, and cover the two main peculiarities in written English – two-letter sounds, and the effect of the 'magic' letters 'e', 'i' and 'y' on earlier vowels and the consonants 'c' and 'g'. The whole process, plus plenty of reading-aloud practice, could be accomplished quite easily in two terms, I had discovered; an article to this effect winged its way to *Special Children* magazine. They promptly despatched a photographer to record us in action at our after school sessions (parents, grandparents, youngsters and me). The resulting piece really did us proud, and for several months following its publication I was inundated by requests for my phonic word card packs.

One correspondent was Pam Clark, Learning Support teacher at Longniddry. She had been looking for a 'user friendly' phonics programme for a long time, and liked my approach because it dovetailed so well with the use of 'real books' for reading. She set to work enthusiastically, and in a very short time the whole school was buzzing with the success of her pupils, formerly strugglers, but rapidly becoming strugglers no longer. The programme was far too good to keep to itself, Longniddry decided: the teachers made a video about it, and Pam began visiting other schools in the area to talk about her work.

Meanwhile, down in deepest Devon, I was torn between delight at the progress of my own secondary level students, and frustration that they had floundered about for so long before getting appropriate help. "If only I could have done this with you when you were five," I kept thinking, watching yet another child romping through books of his own choice, and reading them aloud with confidence. "You wouldn't even have the problems now – and you could have avoided all that heart-ache and misery in primary school." Most of my pupils did indeed make spectacular leaps forward, but there were always some who had been so damaged by their earlier experiences that they had lost belief in themselves, and shunned anything to do with reading and writing.

I was hatching my 'as if' scheme – teach all children, from Reception and upwards, *as if* they were dyslexic. But how was I going to persuade primary schools to take the idea on board, when I was a mere Literacy Support teacher at secondary level?

Two things were vital, I decided. I had to offer class teachers colourful picture books to supplement the packs of phonic word cards, and so make the programme more enticing for small children. Then I had to find a school willing to trial the approach with its Reception pupils.

The angels must have been with me, because both challenges were resolved almost before I articulated them to myself. I was blessed with a dedicated Classroom Assistant, Dawn Chase, who not only went the second mile in every lesson at school – she had also decided that my phonic programme was just the thing for her own children. Unbeknownst to me, she had persuaded an artist friend, with small children of her own, to illustrate the alphabet words, and the words containing two-letter sounds; the two mothers were happily teaching their own children at home, using cards plus picture books, and making similar steady advances. At length Dawn brought the books in to school, to show me. I could hardly speak. The pictures were better than anything I could have imagined: bold, humorous, clear, colourful, and as far as I could tell, quite irresistible to children. In great excitement, I went round to see the artist, Debbie Smith, to ask her if I could use her drawings, and would she please please do some more to illustrate the 'alphabet magic' story (the saga of the magic letters)? Debbie fell to with a will – and I had my three picture books.

Then I approached Pam Clark to find out if Longniddry would consider introducing the programme with mainstream classes, and much younger children.

The school was doubtful at first. This was partly because the approach had been so successful with special needs children, using individual tuition, that the staff found it difficult to envisage transferring it to entire classes. However, they were willing to give it a go, and with typical Scottish thoroughness they set up two groups of Primary One (=Reception) children: an experimental class, using my 'Alphabet Magic' approach, and a control group following a more traditional phonic programme.

They started at the beginning of the academic year, in September. The books at that stage were in black and white, and Longniddry staff painstakingly coloured them in, laminated them, and also produced smaller versions of the coloured pictures, which the children could peg onto 'washing' lines stretched across the classroom.

By Christmas the school had run into problems. My heart sank when Pam reported this at the other end of the phone. What was the trouble? "Well," said Pam, sounding deliberately gloomy, "the experimental group – 'your' group – is so far ahead of the control group that we don't feel it's morally right not to use the programme with the control group as well. But then we won't be able to make a scientific comparison."

The inward grin reached from my toes to the top of my head. "Oh yes," I replied. "Do it with all the children. Compare the results with national norms, and that will be just as scientific."

The lovely thing about Longniddry's investigation was that the whole school took it on board, not just the two Primary One teachers (Sarah Morrice and Shona Larnie), and Pam herself. Everybody helped with the colouring in, and the laminating. A classroom assistant, Jennifer Cummings, and her pupils constructed a glorious Alphabet Wizard, almost as big as the children, who went from class to class to lend his benign presence to the telling of the 'Alphabet Magic' story. The Primary One teachers invented games, accompanied by guitar playing, to make the learning process more fun. Teachers further up the school started incorporating bits of the programme. And perhaps most important of all, the headteacher, Ann McLanachan, threw herself into the endeavour heart and soul. Every day a new and mysterious word went up on her office door, at child height, and the pupils would line up to work it out. They whispered the word in Ann's ear, and were rewarded with a hug and a sticker.

Everyone involved with the programme – teachers, parents, children – seemed to make the same delighted discovery: that it belonged to them in particular. Most also decided that they had to hand it on to as many other people as possible, usually embellished with some contribution of their own.

There were one or two unexpected snags. A parent recounted her embarrassment when taking her little boy round a shopping mall. He had a deep, carrying voice, even though he had just finished Primary One. "Mum," he demanded excitedly, "can we go and see that film, 'Aus-tin Pow-ers, The Spy Who Shagged Me'?" – pointing to a large poster nearby. "Er – no," said Mum shortly, "it's a 12." But she could not escape the inevitable question. "Mum – what does 'shagged' mean?" Mum took refuge in cowardice, as any sensible parent would. "I don't know," she said, trying to avoid the interest of other shoppers, "maybe they've got the wrong word." Ten minutes later, when she thought the question had been forgotten, Calum declared suddenly, "Snatched! – that must have been what they meant. 'The Spy Who Snatched Me'."

A father who was present at the same meeting explained how he had speedily escorted his own little boy from a public toilet, when the youngster started trying to sound out the f*** word, scrawled on one of the walls.

(Maybe the programme has to come with a public health warning – children who complete it will assume that *all* words, wherever they occur, are their own personal property, amenable to the same sounding out technique...)

Two years later, Longniddry was inspected. It received a glowing report on the literacy front, and rather than giving advice to the school, on how things could be improved, the inspectors decided to give advice to the local council instead. "Something very exciting is happening at Longniddry," they said. "You must spread it around."

So the council rescued me from my black and white photocopying, and spiral binding. They published the whole thing in colour, together with Longniddry's games and other additions, and made *Alphabet Magic: The Tallying Approach to Phonics* official recommended policy in primary schools throughout East Lothian.

Like most good programmes, it isn't teacher proof. It does depend on the commitment and dedication of the staff who implement it. But when all primary teachers tackle their job of teaching literacy, in the unwavering belief that entry to the world of written language is the birthright of every single child, there is no limit to what all children can achieve.

We have only to will the means. The children will take care of the rest.

Appendix 1

Year Plan
Total literacy, for all children, in one year

Total literacy, for all children, in one year

Making the shift to an 'experience' approach (from an 'academic' one) requires a fundamental change in our thinking about literacy. Reading and writing involve nothing more than a series of operations on print – seeing meanings in written words; following the text from left to right and from page to page; tallying written words with spoken words, bit by bit; forming letters yourself and thinking of both the meanings of the words, and their matching sounds, while you write them. Then there are other procedures which support these basic ones: learning alphabetical order so as to use conventional dictionaries; finding your way around in a spelling dictionary; typing skills. Brain Gym exercises help all children to learn more efficiently, and it is important to make coloured overlays available for any child who might need them (see Chapter VI).

And that's it, really!

Our job as teachers is to provide abundant experience in these areas, and to monitor each child's journey from dependence on others to help him carry out the operations, to full and enjoyable independence.

We can accomplish this, for all children, in a single year. The first step is to demonstrate the procedures, then give the children the experience of using the procedures, then make sure they practise until the procedures have become instinctive. If we realize a particular child is struggling, we step in immediately with a bit more help, and a lot more practice, until he isn't struggling any more.

The approach means that we can always offer material at a child's interest level (rather than his 'ability' level). We may certainly use reading schemes, alongside 'real books', if we want to, so long as no child stays stuck on a particular title, or a particular scheme.

Acknowledging the difference between the two reading processes helps as well. If a child adores *The Enormous Crocodile* (or *Harry Potter* if he's older), fine, read these books to him whenever he likes, encouraging him to follow the print while you read. He reads back a paragraph or so when you've finished. This activity is a brilliant way of helping him to see the meanings in a steadily growing vocabulary of written words.

Use simpler texts when your main concern is to help a child practise reading aloud. You can start off reading a page to him first, then he reads it back; but, increasingly, as he works through the phonic programme, ask him to try reading on his own, from scratch, scrutinizing each word, and making sure he matches the right sounds to all the letters. Even if he makes mistakes (which you correct), this experience provides a brilliant foundation for his later independent writing – as well as helping him to find out the meanings of written words by himself.

Because you are not working through a particular set of reading materials, but rather concentrating on teaching procedures, you can cover the following plan with children of any age. The ideal is probably Reception year in an English primary school, or Primary One in Scotland. (Start at the beginning of the Spring Term if entry is staggered due to age.)

The easiest way of implementing the plan is by using my phonic programme, *Alphabet Magic – The Tallying Approach to Phonics*, published by East Lothian Council, John Muir House, Haddington EH41 3HA. Tel: 01620 82 7433. The programme is outlined in three books: *Book One, The Alphabet Book*; *Book Two, The Book of Combinations* (two-letter sounds), and *Book Three, The Story of Alphabet Magic*. Their *Teacher's Pack* contains a wealth of coloured pictures and words for classroom use, photocopiable record sheets, and Longniddry's *Teacher's Notes* describing the games and activities developed at the school. A video of children in action at Longniddry is included in the *Reference Pack*. See *Books and Materials*, p. 177.

TERM ONE

Brain Gym

Brain Gym exercises (see Chapter VI, pp. 115-117) help with each separate physical activity employed in reading and writing, so use them regularly with all children throughout the school.

1st Half Term

Seeing meanings in written words

Help the children to understand whole written words. Stick words in large thick lower case letters (preferably red) on objects around the room (wall, door, window, table, chair, books, mirror, plant etc.). This enables most of your pupils to form really clear visual images of the words. Point them out and say them to the children quite often. 'Test' the youngsters by asking "Show me the word that says…" (rather than "What is this word?"). Make sure all the children end up getting the words right, and praise them for every success.

Read 'big books' to the class, while the children follow the print, pointing to the words as you go along. Invite parents in to read books to individual children or small groups, again holding the books so the youngsters can follow the print. Encourage and help the children to identify interesting words and phrases from time to time.

It is an excellent idea to have a bank of word cards for the reading books in current use. (Enlist parents or grandparents to help – grandparents especially are often delighted to be involved in such an undertaking.) Big sheets of card 78cm by 52cm cut up into 64 cards 4.8cm by 13cm. Use thick marking pens, navy or dark green rather than black, and cream card (not white), for the benefit of children with Irlen Syndrome. Print the word as it appears in the book on one side of the card, and slightly altered on the reverse. E.g. **and/And, shoe/shoes, the/They**,

should/shouldn't, thing/nothing, worse/WORSE, here/there, here/Where. (The last two cards enable you to explain the three 'place' words – all ending in 'here' – which some children find confusing. 'Here' = 'in this place', 'there' = 'in that place', 'where' = 'in which place'.) At first you tell the child the word on the front, and help him to read the version on the back. At later sessions encourage him to read both sides of the card from memory. Then he reads the relevant pages in the book.

Word cards like these have numerous advantages. As you progress through the phonic programme, help a child to sound out the words on the front of the cards. Two-letter sounds can be printed in red, to aid recognition, and so can the 'magic' letters 'e', 'i' and 'y', if this stage has been reached. You can even use the cards to explain quite complicated ideas – e.g. when the only vowel in a one-syllable word comes at the end, it ordinarily says its alphabet name (**he, she, be, go, no, ho**). Add a consonant (**hop**), and the vowel says its sound name. But then add a magic letter, and the vowel says its alphabet name again (**hope, hoping**). You will be surprised to find how quickly children can absorb such information, and start using the same vocabulary themselves – even pointing out the exceptions (**do, to, the**) with delight.

'Irregular' words can be included straightaway, and usually you can show the children how to sound out these words as well (e.g. thŭ, thor, thought).

Then when a child reads the pages in the book, he will progress much more quickly because he doesn't have to stop and 'work out' the words on the page, he only has to recognize them (although you can help him to sound out any words he has forgotten). It's a good idea if he reviews the words and re-reads the last few pages covered, before learning new words and new pages.

Again, parents and grandparents can be involved in the activity, at home or at school, working with one child or small groups of youngsters who are all tackling the same book.

(Notice that this is a very far cry from a 'look-and-say' procedure, when a child is expected to learn all the words in a reader before reading it himself, and can stay stuck on a particular book for weeks or even months. You are not 'testing' the children, but giving them the experience of recognizing the words, often sounding them out, and following an interesting text. All the time you are making sure the children *succeed* continually, so 'failure' just doesn't exist.)

Such a bank of word cards may be used in all sorts of ways. When the children are first getting going with reading, you can make sentences from the reading books with the cards. Ask the children to give you the words you need, then they read the sentences from left to right. Point out the same sentences when a child reads the book by himself.

The *Breakthrough to Literacy* materials, published by Longman, offer a similar kind of word-by-word approach. They include a large-sized teacher's stand and magnetic word tiles, for shared sentence-level work, while the smaller pupil's sentence-maker allows for individual work including writing.

Many of these activities can be continued for the first year or so. But make especial provision for reading to the children, while they follow the print, throughout their time at primary school.

The 'Tallying' approach to sounding out words

The Alphabet Book – Book One
Step 1 – 1st sound onto left hand edge
Go through the *Alphabet Book* with the children.
*Identify the object in the picture.
*Say the whole words opposite.

*Isolate the first sound in the spoken word. ("'Apple' begins with 'ă', doesn't it – can you hear that?")

*Map the sound onto the red letter at the left hand edge of the written word. ("The sound 'ă' goes with that red letter over there. The small letter says 'ă', and this capital letter says 'ă' as well.")

*"Now you can say the red letters by themselves," [pointing to the letters underneath the picture] "that says 'ă' and that says 'ă'."
The children copy this procedure until all are getting it right.

Repeat with the other 25 words in the *Alphabet Book*, teaching one letter a day. Review several letters already covered before introducing a new one.

Notice that the children are learning the common sounds for the letters of the alphabet as a *by-product* of learning and practising the 'tallying' technique. See Longniddry's *Teacher's Notes* for ideas about games providing further practice.

Writing the letters
Teach the children to write each letter as it is introduced, in a cursive script. (See Chapter V, 'Ways around the blockages', pp. 90-91, for a Cursive Handwriting Sheet, and an explanation of why cursive handwriting is so helpful for dyslexics especially.)

Use handwriting paper, printed in 'tram lines'. (Photocopiable masters are included in a Handwriting Folder, available from me, which also supplies lists of all the phonic words in cursive writing for tracing and copying.) Handwriting paper makes it much easier for the children to produce writing of a uniform size, from the outset. I have seen so much truly awful writing at secondary level – the direct result of an 'emergent writing' policy in the Infant School – when it is much more difficult to put it right. Teaching a beautiful and legible script at the start does not stifle the children's creativity, because they can dictate to adults, and have ample experience of copying, before we expect them to write out their own original work from scratch. See Term Three in this Plan.

Some letters in the cursive script have to be altered slightly so that they can be written without lifting the pencil:

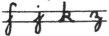

(The letter 'x' is the only exception to this, having two separate strokes.)

You need an initial stroke for each letter, so that it can always begin in the same place:

a rainbow for round beginning letters

or a rocker for straight beginning letters

Help the children to describe these initial strokes while they produce them. A rainbow 'starts on the bottom line, goes up to the top line, and round to the dot':

A short rocker 'starts with a rocky bit on the bottom line, goes straight up to the top line, and back down again':

A tall rocker is 'twice as tall as a short rocker':

Then the children can help you decide how to turn 'rainbows' and 'rockers' into letters of the alphabet. A good way to start is by making a row of 'rainbows' into a row of 'waves':

The children will almost certainly spot that this is also a row of ' *c*'s. They should practise the 'waves' until they are reasonably fluent.

To change a wave into an '*a*', start on the bottom line, up to the top line, do the curly bit at the top of the wave, backtrack right round, straight up to the top line, and down:

A '*b*' starts with a tall rocker, straight down, straight back up to the top line, and right round. A '*d*' starts with a rainbow/wave, backtrack right round, tall leg and down. A '*p*' starts with a short rocker, long leg, up to the top line, and right round. And so on. Review letters already learned by asking your pupils to describe them in this way, and you will find this really helps them to write the letters accurately.

As soon as you reach '*d*', you can show the children how to join letters together to produce a proper word. Write the three letters '*b*' '*a*' and '*d*' on the blackboard, separately, but quite close together. Add the joining strokes in a different colour:

Explain that when we join from the bottom of a letter, we have a 'u' shaped connector. This avoids the letters being too spread out. Later on, when you reach 'o', you will point out that we join from the top of a letter by using a 'saucer' connector:

The children should practise tracing over the letters

then add the joining strokes, before writing the word as a whole. They need lots of experience in tracing whole words before writing the words by themselves.

Pupils can write all the *Set 1* words in my phonic programme – and any others they encounter – as soon as they have learned the relevant letters.

(Remember that the initial strokes described can be abandoned later, if the pupil wishes, but they are very helpful for learning the letter forms, at the beginning.)

Some children have great physical difficulty with handwriting. Continue providing these youngsters with ample experience of 'aided' writing, as described above. In addition, you can teach all your pupils typing skills, using the proper fingers. See Chapter V, pp. 92-94.

Steps 2 and 3 – matching the ends and middles
The next step on the phonic front is to show the children how the whole spoken word matches the whole written word, so that the last sound in the spoken word maps onto the right hand edge of the written word. You demonstrate this by pointing to a written word and saying it aloud, stressing the last sound and pointing to the final letter/s.

Teach the children to map sounds onto all the *Set 1* words (see *Appendix 2*), moving from left to right, and blending the sounds as they go along. (So they would sound out 'frog' by saying 'fŭ, frŭ, frŏ, frog', not 'fŭ, rŭ, ŏ, gŭ'.)

Show the word 'bad', saying, "This word says 'bad'," emphasizing the 'du' sound and pointing to the 'd'. Cover the 'ad', and say "Now it says 'bŭ." Uncover the 'a'. "Now it says 'bă'." Uncover the 'd'. "Now it says 'bad'. You do it." Different children repeat the sounds while you uncover the letters. (The *Set 1a* words are printed like this on the reverse of the cards in my phonic word card packs: b ba bad, j ja jazz, etc. This makes it very easy for you to teach the tallying technique.)

Help the children to write the word 'bad' in large cursive handwriting. (See above.) Initially, the children sound out the words whenever they trace or copy them.

Carry out these activities with about three new words a day. You can sound out any word as soon as you have taught the relevant letters. Encourage the children to sound out the words learned the previous day, from memory, i.e. without looking at the words. (This is what you want them to do when writing.) They can also spell the words using coloured plastic letters – lower case – again building up the sounds while they choose the letters.

Practising when reading
Now when you have finished reading an exciting story to the class, children could volunteer to identify words they can sound out; then see if they can spell them without looking, saying the sound names of the letters if they don't know the alphabet names.

A child can also be encouraged to read back to an adult a couple of paragraphs from a story just read to him, as already described. He should never 'guess' or 'predict'. Tell him any words he cannot remember. He repeats them correctly and carries on. But if he hesitates over a short-vowel-sound word, help him to sound it out. (As his reading becomes more fluent, he will indeed learn the meanings of many new words by reading them, but you don't have to teach him the procedure, he will do it automatically. Sounding out these new words will then supply his speaking vocabulary.)

Don't worry if not all children are remembering everything. So long as they practise continually, learning is steadily taking place – and as soon as a particular letter has been introduced, all literacy activities will reinforce its use.

2nd Half Term

The Book of Combinations – Book Two (two-letter sounds)

Work through *The Book of Combinations* in the same way (teaching these two-letter sounds: ai, ay, au, aw, ch, ea, ee, er, ir, ur, ar, or, ew, ng, oo, ou, ow, oa, ph, sh, th, ui).

*Identify the object in the picture.

*Say the whole word opposite.

*Point to the red letters in the word, and say the sound they match in that particular word. "Look – those red letters go together, and say 'ai'. Can you hear the sound 'ai' in the word 'train'?" The children copy you.

*Help the children to say the same sound for the combination printed by itself underneath the picture.

*After a while, encourage the children to go through the book (or separate pictures) by themselves, just saying the sounds for the letter combinations printed underneath the pictures.

*Help the children to sound out the words in the book, and on word cards. (Say 'tŭ, trŭ, trai, train', not 'tŭ, trŭ, tră, trai, train'.)

*Teach the children to write the same words, in joined writing, sounding them from memory while they write.

Also, point out and practise words containing two-letter sounds from reading books, as you go along. A child may now be able to start tackling unfamiliar text (large clear print) – with lots of help from you to make sure he gets the words right. Enlist parents and grandparents to make banks of word cards for popular books: well worth the time and effort. (See p. 146.) Tell a young reader any 'irregular' or difficult words immediately, but then show him how to sound them out. This means that you can use 'real books' as reading books, from the beginning, but your pupils are still learning to read them accurately as well as fluently.

TERM TWO

The Story of Alphabet Magic – Book Three

This is the term for the story of Alphabet Magic. See Longniddry's *Teacher's Notes* for the story itself, and suggestions for tackling the *Set 3* words. (Or, the story is outlined in my booklet *As Easy as ABC: Phonic Analysis in Two Terms.*) Continue with reading practice, as above.

TERM THREE

All the basic groundwork has now been covered. The children have learned how to invest written words with meanings, and to read stories and books by doing this.

They have learned the whole process of phonic 'translation' – how to map spoken words onto written words, working from left to right, and building up the sounds as they go along (*Book One*).

They have learned about the two main 'peculiarities' of the English phonetic system:

a) that more than one letter can match a single sound (*Book Two*)

b) that when certain letters (mainly 'e', 'i' and 'y') occur in certain positions in words, the sounds matching earlier letters can alter (*Book Three*).

They have learned to recognize, sound out and write correctly at least 120 words which illustrate these processes.

As a result, they are now able to read aloud *any* material that is at their interest level!

In Term Three, all that remains is to consolidate and practise their new found skills, and extend their literacy competence in the following areas: independent reading aloud, spelling, using 'spelling' and 'meaning' dictionaries, and independent writing.

Independent reading aloud

Accurate reading aloud is the best possible basis for accurate writing, spelling and punctuation skills. Punctuation marks provide a wealth of information to the reader-*aloud* – when to pause in the middle (comma) or at the end of an idea (full stop), when to change the voice because someone is speaking (speech marks), when to have a longer pause at the end of a paragraph, etc. Someone who has had abundant practice in reading aloud will have little difficulty in using punctuation signs correctly in his/her own writing.

Reading aloud is also an excellent basis for spelling skills, because the more you read aloud, the more closely the spoken words stick to the written words. Writing involves the reverse process – you say the words to yourself, 'silently' or aloud, and the words you put on the page match these spoken words 'in the head'. So if you have already learned to match written words with spoken words, bit by bit, while reading, it is much easier to match the same words, bit by bit, while writing.

(Reading silently does not draw the attention to punctuation signs, or correct spelling, in the same way, which is one reason why the conventional 'whole language' approach causes such problems with writing as the children move up the school.)

It is therefore very important that all children should continue to practise reading aloud throughout their school careers. It may be tempting just to let them get on with silent reading once you know they can do it, but making adequate provision for reading aloud as well as silent reading will pay off in spades when it comes to writing.

Continue helping your pupils to read new books by way of the word cards mentioned earlier. This ensures a strong grasp of the vocabulary, and confident word attack skills, without impeding fluency or enjoyment of the text.

But you may well find that many youngsters can manage some books by now without the aid of word cards. It's a good plan to start the undertaking with books that are already familiar: then the child isn't groping for the meaning, only practising linking meaningful print with meaningful speech. He has all the techniques, so he won't find it threatening to be asked to do this. On the contrary, he will be delighted to discover and revel in his ability.

Choose a book in nice clear print that he has followed previously, maybe identifying some of the interesting words after it was read to him. Now ask him to read it aloud to you (or anyone else available). He mustn't guess, but look closely at every word and tally it in his head before reading it. If he flounders, don't let him struggle, but tell him what the word says, and show him how it tallies. He repeats the word correctly, and carries on. A child can tackle several familiar books in this fashion.

Then he moves on to the unfamiliar ones. If you want to use a reading scheme at this point, go ahead, because this is where reading schemes come into their own. They are designed to give children cumulative practice in reading aloud independently. You can use phonic reading schemes, or look-and-say reading schemes, or a mix of both – a child can manage either equally well. Don't start at the very beginning of the scheme, but select a title at the pupil's interest level, and carry on from there, moving as quickly as possible so he doesn't get bored. (It's the amount of practice that matters.)

If you don't want to use reading schemes, you can stay with real books. Notice that the Dr Seuss books, for example, would certainly qualify as 'real' books in terms of content, interest and illustrations, but are also strongly based on phonics, so would be a good choice at this point.

Help a youngster to read unfamiliar books in the same way as the familiar ones – i.e. give him as much help as he needs to get it right.

Don't abandon the custom of reading to the children, while they follow the print, just because they are becoming established as independent readers. You can help them to move on to much more advanced texts in this way.

Children should continue to practise the two sorts of reading (silent reading and reading aloud) throughout their primary school years – and probably beyond. There are many different sensible reasons you can use for asking them to read aloud – reading their own stories to a group, rehearsing for reading in assembly, play reading (record on tape), reading to smaller children, and so on. But no child will feel demoralized when you ask him to read aloud, because you have made sure that he already knows how.

Spelling

The 'word jumblers' cannot learn to spell by means of 'look, cover, write, check' because their mental images of words are unstable and unreliable. This is why sounding out written words is so crucially important for dyslexics, because it enables them to match the word on the page with the relatively stable spoken 'engram' of the word in the head, thus bypassing the perceptual blockage. It is the key to accurate reading, and also accurate spelling. If dyslexics learn to 're-say' any irregular word, in accordance with its spelling, they will be able to spell as confidently as anybody else.

There are only three steps to building up a 'saying-for-spelling' vocabulary, and one of the three steps will work for any possible word, no matter how irregular. (See the *Key to Sound Spelling*, p. 80.) The *Key to Sound Spelling* is useful as a backup for *all* children, however, not just dyslexics, so it makes sense to teach it to all children, right from the start. The Key can be operated in conjunction with 'look, cover, write, check', because you are simply incorporating one additional, vital step – i.e. 'look, *re-say if necessary*, cover, write, check'.

The Key to Sound Spelling, Step 1

Your pupils are already using Step 1 in the Key (sounding out regular words) as a result of working through the phonic programme. Just remind them to sound out words in their heads whenever they write, matching letters to sounds. (This avoids mistakes like 'forg' for 'frog' on the part of the word jumblers.)

Step 2

Step 2 involves re-saying words in line with their spelling. (Nearly all of us use this procedure with 'Wed-nes-day' and some other words.) The children need to learn to spot the three 'sneaks', and to think of spelling cues which will sort them out.

You can help your pupils to do this by going back to the alphabet words introduced at the outset. The children read the words aloud first, then scrutinize each word to see if they can spot any sneaks. (Keep reminding them what to look out for – silent letters, double letters, or letters making a different sound.) If there are no sneaks, the youngsters should spell the words aloud orally, tallying them in their heads while they spell. In the case of sneaks, they need to think of cues which will remind them of the spelling. E.g. for 'apple' they could say 'ap-p-lē', for 'dragon' 'drag-ŏn', for 'nurse' 'You are [to remind about the 'ur'!] a nurs-ē', etc. They think of the cues while they spell the words aloud.

After this, they practise writing all the words, either tallying them straight off, or saying the cues first, then tallying the chunks. (A photocopiable work sheet is included in the East Lothian pack of record sheets.)

Step 3

Not all words fall neatly into resayable chunks. (E.g. 'thought', 'would', 'night', 'laughed'.) For these words, the children need to use mnemonics to deal with the awkward bits. See the *Key to Sound Spelling*, Step 3. Sometimes you can teach mnemonics for whole words, e.g. '*b*ig *e*lephants *c*an't *a*lways *u*se *s*mall *e*ntrances' for 'because'; but try to use Step 2 in preference whenever possible, or a mnemonic for just the difficult part of a word, then the same mnemonic can be used for all 'ough' words, etc. A work sheet for teaching Step 3 is also included in the pack of record sheets.

The ACE Spelling Dictionary

Conventional dictionaries can be daunting for the word jumblers. How do you set about finding a word in a dictionary if you're not sure what it looks like? The *ACE* (Aurally Coded English) *Spelling Dictionary*, published by LDA, has been designed to overcome this problem – a youngster can track down the spelling of any word by sounding it out.

If you teach all your pupils to use the ACE Dictionary, then any word jumblers will be able to do so when the need arises. Other children can use it if they wish, or opt for a 'meaning' dictionary instead, the choice is theirs. But practice in using the ACE Dictionary encourages a child to think carefully about the sounds in words, the number of syllables, and the difference between vowels and consonants; which is beneficial for any youngster's spelling skills.

Detailed suggestions for showing a whole class how to use the Dictionary are included in the East Lothian pack of record sheets.

A 'meaning' dictionary

Using a conventional dictionary requires different kinds of skills. It is best consulted when a child already knows the spelling of a word, and wants to find out the meaning. Again, see the pack of record sheets for suggestions about class work to teach this skill.

Extended writing

The children are so used to sounding out words while they write that this has probably become automatic and instinctive by now – which is what you want. So long as the spoken words are properly matched to their equivalent written words, they will 'hold the written words in place' in each child's head, making it very easy for him to remember how to spell them. (This happens even with the so-called 'irregular' words, as we have already noted.)

So carry on making sure that your pupils sound out all words, whenever they write. After a while they will be able to do this inside their heads, rather than out loud.

The next step on the writing front is to put words together, and generate running text. The youngsters aren't yet quite ready to do so independently – but they soon will be if they have the experience of copying, to begin with.

There are many practical and creative ways of arranging for this to happen. The children can contribute to an oral story, recorded on tape. You write out extracts, in cursive script, and give a photocopy to each child. He traces over it, first. Then you show your pupils how to copy it, so that they learn the spellings.

They must never copy letter by letter, always word by word. They look at each word, think of spelling cues if necessary, and then write it from memory, either tallying straight through the word, or tallying the cues.

Review the passage with the children before they copy it. Decide as a group whether each word comes under Step 1, 2 or 3 in the *Key to Sound Spelling*, and what the cues could be. (Each child can use these cues, or think of his own if he prefers, or even use none at all if he can manage without. But all the children should sound out all the words while they write them, then immediately check to make sure the spellings are correct. As already noted, they are using the 'look, cover, write, check' procedure, just expanding it to re-say the words when appropriate.)

You could import a whole class of nine-year-olds for half an hour or so. Each five-year-old dictates his story to an older child, who writes it out in a neat cursive script, correctly spelled. (This is an excellent reason for the older child to write neatly and accurately.) The five-year-old trances over it (if he wishes), copies it as described, and perhaps illustrates it as well.

Notice that every child has expressed himself freely, without having to interrupt the flow of his ideas by constantly seeking correct spellings. But he has still ended up with a technically correct version, and is steadily adding to his 'saying-for-spelling' vocabulary in the process.

There is nothing wrong with giving the children poems and short stories by their favourite authors to copy. This provides abundant practice in 'how to do it'. As a result, when the children move on to independent writing, they will manage it easily because they have already served their apprenticeship.

And now you can begin to nudge them in this direction. Suppose a child is bubbling over with a story, but there is no scribe available just then. "Try writing it out by yourself, Robert – I bet you know most of the words, but you can always ask if you get stuck. How does it begin, 'Once upon a time there was a baby dragon' – oh, go on, you can manage that! Don't forget to put in full stops, capital letters and speech marks, the way you do when you're copying." So Robert sits down and has a bash – and lo and behold, there are the words coming out of his fingers, and he knows how to write them, and he knows how to spell them.

The transition from copying to original, independent writing is happening seamlessly and naturally for every child.

Scotopic Sensitivity (Irlen) Syndrome

Remember that all children should be screened for this condition at seven, and again at eleven, to make sure of identifying every sufferer. See Chapter VI, pp. 118-120.

Monitoring progress

As Doman points out, 'children love to learn, but they do not love to be tested' – because testing puts them on the spot, with the ever-present risk of failing. Liz Waterland suggests measuring 'degrees of success', rather than degrees of failure; and it is quite possible to do this in a way that gives you all the information you need about the level of each child's experience so far.

For example, my phonic programme is divided into six steps, from knowing the sound-names for the letters of the alphabet, to knowing the six magic spells, and being able to sound out and spell orally the relevant words. There are four boxes for each step on the child's record sheet. You initial the first box when he can manage the procedure with considerable help: he gets a '4', with the date, when he can carry it out independently. Eventually he must score a '4' for every step, but he can start working on Step 2 even before he has earned his '4' for Step 1. When he has a string of '4's, all the way down, he is given a Certificate for 'Foundation Phonics'. Other record sheets demonstrate his progress in the other literacy areas.

One positive aspect of this approach to record keeping is that parents can so easily be involved. They might as well have copies of the record sheets at home, informing the school when their child has earned a '2' or a '3' for a particular step. The teacher needs to check before awarding the '4', but that is all good consolidation.

Another useful feature is that it is very straightforward to fill in the gaps for a child who is a late arrival at the school, or who has been absent for any length of time, again involving parents, classroom assistants, and/or classmates.

External tests are a fact of life, necessary for other purposes; but this way of monitoring progress will go a long way towards ensuring that your pupils can take such hurdles in their stride, and perform creditably when tests are required.

If you are working with a child at home, you can obtain a separate pack of 'Notes and Record Sheets' directly from me. (See *Books and materials*, p. 176.)

It's quite true. Any child can become fully literate in a single year. No, he may not be reading about the second law of thermodynamics. But he will be able to understand print, read aloud, write neatly and spell accurately, at his interest level.

Well, that'll do for starters.

Appendix 2

The Sound Spelling Vocabularies

Here is a list of all the words in my phonic word card packs. There are two sets of alphabet words – one for primary level, and an advanced set for secondary level, when you want to make sure that the youngster knows the sound names for all the letters of the alphabet, without feeling patronized by a juvenile vocabulary. Some of the words in the secondary level set have been deliberately chosen because they can be split into prefix and root. E.g. astro-naut = star sailor, com-puter = thinking together with, kilo-gram = 1000 grams, micro-chip = very small chip, television = pictures from far away. You can encourage the student to track down other words with the same prefixes: very good for comprehension and for spelling.

The Alphabet Set – Primary Level 26 cards
apple, banana, camel, dragon, elephant, fox, grandmother, helicopter, ink, jam, king, lion, mountain, nurse, octopus, palace, queen, rabbit, snake, tree, umbrella, volcano, witch, x-ray, yeti, zebra

The Alphabet Set – Secondary Level 26 cards
astronaut, battleship, computer, dragon, electricity, flying saucer, galaxy, helicopter, ink, jet engine, kilogram, laser, microchip, nucleus, oxygen, programme, quarter, robot, snake, television, umbrella, video, witch, x-ray, yeti, zebra crossing

Sound Spelling Set 1 – Vowel Sandwiches 50 cards
Set 1a
bad, jazz, mad, sat, van; bed, fell, red, web, yes; big, him, kit, lid, pig; cog, doll, fox, got, top; bus, cup, nut, sun, tub

166

Set 1b

grab, hand, slam; desk, lend, nest; kilt, quiz, twig; blot, frog, smog; jump, plug, tusk; scram, exact; quest, request; crisp, strip; frost, clock; trust, strum

Sound Spelling Set 2 – The Combinations 36 cards
Set 2a

train, crayon, astronaut, claw, children, beach, three, helicopter, third, nurse, star, morning, jewels, king, coal, Typhoo (kangaroo), book, mouth, tower, elbow, graph, shampoo, cloth, fruit

Set 2b

(The combinations are not printed in red. The child identifies the combination/s, then sounds out the word.)
proud, bring, drown, play, flew, sprang, squeak, splash, shrink, scream, other, mother

Sound Spelling Set 3 – Alphabet Magic 34 cards
Spell 1 – The magic 'e' spell

     made, grate, snake; these, scene; kite, shine, slide;
     hope, clothes, phone; tube, exclude, fortune

Spell 2 – The magic 'i' and magic 'y' spell

     hoping, shining, shiny

Spell 3 – Consonants can't use magic

     hopeful, grateful, hopeless

Spell 4 – The double defence

     trotting, hopping, muddy, webbed

Spell 5 – Changing 'c's and 'g's

     ceiling, city, cygnet; gentle, giant, gypsy

Spell 6 – The bodyguard 'u'

     guess, guide, plague, guy

Many children enjoy typing out the magic spells, using colours of their own choice for the headings, and red for the magic letters (as above). They can be encouraged to add to the lists, and practise explaining how the spells work.

Appendix 3

The 'here, there and everywhere' words

Dyslexics often have particular trouble with annoying words like 'hear' and 'here', there' and 'their', which sound the same, but are spelled differently because they have different meanings. It is useful to teach spelling cues for these words, and review them frequently until they have been mastered.

I start with the word 'ear', using a mnemonic if necessary like 'elephants are rambunctious' (then I can include a little picture of an elephant with large *ears*). Carry on as follows:

'Hearing' words
ear (what you hear with)   =   elephants are rambunctious
hear (what you do with your ears)   =   h/ear
heard (what you did with your ears)   =   hear/d

Place words
here (in this place)   =   her/ē
there (in that place)   =   t/here
where (in which place)   =   w/here

Odds and bobs
their (belonging to them)   =   the/i/r (*I* am the most important person for things to belong to)
they're (they are)   =   the/y, apostrophe, rē
wear (put on clothes)   =   w/ear (picture of someone wearing *ear*-muffs)
were (past tense of 'are')   =   wer/ē, or wē/rē
we're (we are)   =   we, apostrophe, rē
herd (of cows)   =   her/d

Proofreading —
Get it Write

$$P^2 \qquad S^2$$

$$P \quad P \qquad S \quad S$$

Proofread for...

Punctuation   Speech

Paragraphing   Spelling

General Hints

Always proofread *aloud*. (You can 'read aloud' under your breath so that no one else can hear.) In this way, you will notice things that need to be changed, much more readily.

Think about what you are reading. Ask yourself, "Does this say what I want it to say? Does the sentence hang together and make sense?" (If you answer, "No," stop immediately and alter what you have written.)

Use the formula $P^2 S^2$ while you are proofreading. Then you won't forget anything. Two 'P's, for Punctuation and Paragraphing. Two 'S's, for Speech and Spelling.

Proofread for... Punctuation

1. *Full stops and capital letters*. Whenever you would draw breath at the end of a complete idea, put a full stop. It should be a small dot resting on the line, and should not look like a comma. (Notice examples in these sentences.) The next word begins with a capital letter.

2. *Question marks and exclamation marks*. Question marks and exclamation marks have full stops 'built in'. You don't need an extra full stop when you use these punctuation signs.

Look out for the six w/h 'asking' words at the beginning of a sentence: Why, What, When, Where, How, Who. The sentence is almost certainly a question, and must end with a question mark. E.g. Where had the luggage gone?

Look out for verbs at the beginning of a sentence. This is a common way of asking a question. E.g. Has he arrived yet?

Use exclamation marks for emphasis, or if someone is speaking loudly or dramatically. E.g. "I never want to see you again!" she cried.

3. *Commas.* When you pause briefly in the middle of a sentence, and the meaning keeps on going, put a *comma*, not a full stop. Sometimes you can join two or more sentences with words like 'and', 'but' or 'so'. Put a *comma* before the joining word. E.g. He crept into the dark attic, and switched on the light.

4. Names of people and places should begin with *capital letters*. When the words Mum and Dad are used as names, they should also begin with capital letters.

5. Inspect all *apostrophes*.

The letter s, at the end of a noun, has two jobs. Sometimes it tells us 'more than one'. Sometimes it shows possession – belonging. Always decide which job the s is doing, then you will see immediately whether you need an apostrophe or not.

If you have written, 'The vampire's swooped down on the lonely traveller," ask, *"How many vampires?"* (More than one, so the s must be joined on – *no* apostrophe – to show the meaning: vampires.)

If you have written, 'Sandras teeth chattered with fright,' ask, *"How many Sandras?"* (Only one, so the s shows possession, and must be separated by an apostrophe: Sandra's teeth.)

If the s is doing both jobs at once – e.g. 'The lions' den' (more than one lion), the apostrophe goes *after* the s to make this clear.

The apostrophe also does two jobs. Sometimes it helps the letter s to show possession (see above).

Sometimes it shows that letters have been omitted (left out). The apostrophe must always point to the place where the letters are missing. E.g. haven't, I've, we'll, sha'n't. (Sha'n't is short for 'shall not', so two apostrophes are technically correct. However, you will find only one in most modern literature: shan't.)

Notice: it's = it is
        its = belonging to it

172

Proofread for... Paragraphing

6. Arrange your work in *paragraphs*. Imagine it as a television play. Whenever the scene changes, begin a new paragraph. Indent your paragraphs clearly – begin a couple of centimetres away from the margin. All other lines must begin close to the margin. You can have several sentences in one paragraph. In your rough draft, use the proofreading symbol [to mark the beginning of a paragraph. E.g. [The depressing moonscape stretched away to the horizon, nothing but dry, dead rubble.

Proofread for... Speech

7. Think of the initials S C P
    S = Speech marks
    C = Capital letters
    P = Punctuation (and Paragraphing)

S = Speech marks. Words actually being spoken (or thought) must go inside speech marks (just as words being spoken in a comic strip go inside a speech bubble). So put speech marks when someone starts talking, and when they stop. E.g. "I want my letter!" Harry shouted.

Closing speech marks go *after* all other punctuation signs.

C = Capital letters. The beginning of a sentence being spoken must begin with a capital letter, even if it comes after a comma (not a full stop). E.g. Gandalf declared, "He will make an excellent burglar when the time comes."

P = Punctuation. Just before *every* set of speech marks, you must have *either* a full stop, *or* a comma. The full stops should already be in place if you have punctuated your sentences properly. So the rule is, if there is no full stop, put in a comma.

E.g. Harry shouted, "I want my letter!" There is no full stop before the opening set of speech marks, so put a comma after 'shouted'. Or: "He will make an excellent burglar when the time comes," said Gandalf. There is no full stop after 'comes', so you must put a comma.

P = Paragraphing. Think: S C P P! Begin a new paragraph when a different person is going to start speaking. (Imagine the television camera moving from one person to another.) If two people are having a long conversation, you could have a lot of very short paragraphs. Some paragraphs could even have just one word!

E.g. "Yes."

"Is that all you can say?" she screamed.

(Notice the small s for 'she screamed'. You're not beginning a new sentence, even though her words have ended with a question mark.)

You can have several sentences between one 'sixty-six' and one 'ninety-nine'. Don't put the 'ninety-nine' until the person has finished speaking, no matter how many sentences he speaks. If you put – he said – or – she screamed – in the middle, though, you mustn't include these words inside the speech marks. Observe how this is done in the next fiction book you read.

Proofread for... Spelling

8. Inspect all doubtful spellings. Say aloud the word *as you have written it*. Ask yourself, "Does the word say what I want it to say?" E.g. maybe you have written 'hecilopter' for 'helicopter'. Saying what you have written helps you to see what to alter. Then say aloud the word, correctly, while you write it. Tally it in your head. This will help you to get letters for all the sounds, in the right order, and avoid mistakes like 'thnik' for 'think'.

Ask a teacher, or another student, for any spelling you are doubtful about.

Or, use the *ACE Spelling Dictionary*, or a Spellmaster, to check all doubtful words. (Both these aids enable you to track down the spelling of any word, by sounding it out.) When you have found a correct spelling, think of cues which will help you to remember it indefinitely.

174

References

Breakthrough to Literacy – see MacKay, Thompson and Shaub, below.

Clark, Margaret, *Young Fluent Readers*. London: Heinemann, 1976.

Cowling, Keda and Harry, *Toe by Toe*. Baildon: K and H Cowling, 1993.

Craig, Felicity, *The Craft of Writing*. One-to-One Publications, 1996. (See *Books and Materials*, p. 176, for details.)

Davis, Ronald D., *The Gift of Dyslexia*. London: Souvenir Press, 1996.

Dennison, Paul, *Brain Gym* (Teachers' Edition). Edukinesthetics, 1986.

Doman, Glenn, *Teach Your Baby to Read*. London: Jonathan Cape, 1965. (First published 1963.)

Farjeon, Eleanor and Herbert, *Kings and Queens*. London: Jane Nissen Books, 2002. (First published 1932.)

Goodman, Kenneth, 'Reading – a Psycholinguistic Guessing Game' in Singer, H. and Ruddell, R. B., *Theoretical Models of Reading*. Delaware: International Reading Association, 1967.

Hannaford, Carla, *Smart Moves: Why Learning Is Not All In Your Head*. Arlington (USA): Great Ocean, 1995.

Hornsby, Bevé, and Shear, Frula, *Alpha to Omega: The A – Z of Teaching Reading, Writing and Spelling*. London: Heinemann, 1975. (First published 1974.)

Hughes, Felicity (previous name of author), *Reading and Writing Before School*. London: Jonathan Cape, 1971.

Irlen, Helen, *Reading by the Colors*. New York: Avery Publishing, 1991.

Langer, Susanne, *Philosophy in a New Key: A Study in the Symbolism of Reason, Rite and Art*. Cambridge, Massachusetts: Harvard University Press, 1942.

MacKay, Thompson and Shaub, *Breakthrough to Literacy*. Harlow, Essex: Longman, 1970.

McDade, James E., 'A Hypothesis for Non Oral Reading', *The Journal of Educational Research*. Heldref Publications, 1937.

Miles, T. R., *Dyslexia: The Pattern of Difficulties*. London: Granada Publishing, 1983.

Moseley, David, and Nicol, Catherine, *The ACE Spelling Dictionary*. Wisbech, Cambs.: Learning Development Aids, 1986.

Orton, S. T., *Reading, Writing and Speech Problems in Children*. New York: W. W. Norton, 1937.

Peters, Margaret, *Diagnostic and remedial spelling manual*. London: Macmillan Education, 1975.

Pollock, Seton, *The Basic Colour Factor Guide*. London: Heinemann, 1965.

Smith, Frank, *Reading*. Cambridge: Cambridge University Press, 1978.

Smith, Frank, *Understanding Reading: A Psycholinguistic Analysis of Reading, and Learning to Read*. London: Holt, Reinhart & Winston, 1971.

Special Children, a magazine for and about those with barriers to learning. Birmingham: The Questions Publishing Company.

Thompson, Helen, *An Experimental Study of the Beginning Reading of Deaf Mutes*. New York: Columbia University Press, 1927.

Waterland, Liz, *Read With Me: An Apprenticeship Approach to Reading*. Stroud, Glos.: The Thimble Press, 1985.

Wiltshire, Stephen, *Drawings*. London: Orion Publishing, 1987.

Books and materials; useful addresses

Materials available from Felicity Craig, One-to-One Publications, 33 Newcomen Road, Dartmouth, South Devon, TQ6 9BN. (Not through bookshops.) Tel: 01803 834270. Payment with order, or official order form, please. Cheques payable to One-to-One Publications. Overseas customers please add one third of the price given, and send a sterling cheque – thankyou!

Sound Spelling Vocabularies – packs of 146 phonic word cards, teaching the mastery of phonic analysis, plus the sound route to spelling. See Appendix 2 (p. 165) for vocabulary lists. Say whether you want the Primary Level or Secondary Level pack. £5.70 per pack, including postage.

As Easy as ABC: Phonic Analysis in Two Terms – describes how to use the phonic word card packs to teach phonics, at home or in school. £3.50 including postage.

Photocopiable *Handwriting Folder* – contains all the words in the phonic programme for a child to copy in cursive writing, sounding them out at the same time. Primary Level or Secondary Level. £4.50 including postage.

Pack of photocopiable *Record Sheets*, for monitoring every child's progress. £5.50 including postage.

The Craft of Writing – a manual for Key Stage 3 teachers (Year 7+), with photocopiable work sheets on spelling, punctuation, grammar, proofreading, dictionary skills, typing and handwriting. Enables English class teachers to meet all the requirements of the National Curriculum in these areas, with particular respect to the needs of dyslexic students. £12.50 including postage.

Materials available from East Lothian Council, Department of Education and Community Services, John Muir House, Haddington EH41 3HA. Tel: 01620 827433. Please send payment with order, or an official order form.

Alphabet Magic – The Tallying Approach to Phonics

Teacher's Pack – contains:
*The *Alphabet Book* and *The Book of Combinations* in full colour, printed on tough laminated card, and bound, plus the coloured pictures for *The Story of Alphabet Magic*
*Smaller coloured pictures, with letters, from *Books One* and *Two*, suitable for pegging up and handling by children
*Phonic word cards for the three books
**Notes and Record Sheets* (photocopiable)
**Teacher's Notes* – includes the story of Alphabet Magic, plus numerous games and activities developed at Longniddry Primary School to teach and practise the tallying procedures.
Price: £75 + £3.90 p&p

Reference Pack - contains:
*The *Alphabet Book, The Book of Combinations,* and *The Story of Alphabet Magic,* in black and white, together with detailed teaching suggestions – separately, £20 + £1.60 p&p
*Video and *Why Phonics?* booklet – separately £15 + £0.95 p&p
Combined in handy red pack - £35 + £3.65 p&p

Further Reading
As well as books discussed in the text (see *References* for publication details), these titles have recently come to my attention:

Frank, Robert, *The Secret Life of the Dyslexic Child.* Provides parents and professionals with a unique opportunity to experience the world through the eyes and ears of a person with dyslexia. Helps parents to negotiate the minefield of securing adequate provision for their dyslexic children, and lists several addresses and websites. London: Rodale, 2003. First published 2002.

Hannaford, Carla, *Smart Moves: Why Learning Is Not All In Your Head*. Includes a detailed study and evaluation of Brain Gym, and describes additional exercises. Invaluable for interested teachers and parents. Arlington (USA): Great Ocean, 1995.

Useful addresses

The British Dyslexia Association (BDA), 98 London Road, Reading RG1 5AV. Tel: 0118 966 8271. www.bda-dyslexia.org.uk
The BDA calls itself 'the voice of dyslexic people', offering advice, information and help to families, professionals and dyslexic individuals, and working to raise awareness and understanding of dyslexia

The International Dyslexia Association (IDA), 8600 LaSalle Road, Chester Building, Suite 382, Baltimore, MD 21286-2044, USA. Tel: (410) 296-0232. www.interdys.org
The International Dyslexia Association is an international, nonprofit organization dedicated to the study and treatment of dyslexia and maintains a strong presence in educational and scientific communities. The IDA was established to continue the pioneering work of Dr Samuel T. Orton (see *References*).

Scotopic Sensitivity (Irlen) Syndrome. For information and advice, contact Patricia Clayton, West Country Irlen Centre, 123 High Street, Chard, Somerset TA20 1QT. Tel: 01460 65555. UK website: www.irlenuk.com International website: www.irlen.com Research website: www.irlen.org.uk

Longniddry Primary School (Headteacher Ann McLanachan), Kitchener Crescent, Longniddry, East Lothian EH32 OLR. Tel: 01875 853161. Email: longniddry.ps@eastlothian.gov.uk

Audiobooks, Calibre Cassette Library, New Road, Weston Turville, Aylesbury, Bucks HP22 5XQ. Tel: 01296 432339. www.calibre.org.uk

Listening Books, 12 Lant Street, London SE1 1QH. Tel: 020 7407 7476 www.listening-books.org.uk

(Calibre and Listening Books are registered charities that provide audio books in cassette format, operating as postal lending libraries.)

Index

NOTES

NOTES

NOTES

NOTES